SATAN C.

SATAN CAST OUT

A Study in Biblical Demonology

Frederick S. Leahy

THE BANNER OF TRUTH TRUST

THE BANNER OF TRUTH TRUST
3 Murrayfield Road, Edinburgh EH12 6EL
P.O. Box 621, Carlisle, Pennsylvania 17013, U.S.A.

© F. S. Leahy 1975
First published 1975

ISBN 0 85151 234 8

Set in 11-12 pt Walbaum
and printed in Great Britain by
Hazell Watson & Viney Ltd
Aylesbury, Bucks

Contents

INTRODUCTION

The material which is presented in this book was largely gathered in response to a practical need on the foreign Mission field. In co-operation with the Foreign Mission Board of the Reformed Presbyterian Church of Ireland I agreed to make a special study of the subject of Demonology with a view to giving guidance to missionaries who are frequently confronted with the phenomenon of demon-possession. It is undoubtedly the case that the same sinister phenomenon is witnessed in many parts of the world today.

Demonology is discussed in theological colleges only in the most general way. There just is not time to study the subject with any degree of thoroughness. Consequently there is much vagueness and at times error in the Protestant pulpit when Satan and the demons are mentioned. Nothing of any importance has been written on the subject, from a Reformed standpoint, since John L. Nevius, a Presbyterian missionary in China, wrote his *Demon Possession and Allied Themes* in 1894. There has been a steady trickle of Dispensationalist writing on the subject and in recent years a number of books by evangelical writers have appeared. They are mostly superficial in their treatment of the subject. Some of them contain wild and unwarranted statements and a few of them are positively dangerous for the unwary to read. Publishers have sensed a market for such books and in a day when we hear much about extrasensory perception, ouija boards, black witches, exorcism and suchlike, there has been a tendency to rush out books on the occult, spirits and demon-possession which pay scant attention to the Biblical evidence, pander to the sensational and often arrive at unwarranted conclusions.

There is a crying need for an examination of this whole subject *in the light of Scripture alone*, bearing in mind that the Scriptures are our only rule of faith and practice. We are concerned to confess what has been revealed in Scripture and not what is partly the result of logical deduction and subjective opinion. All available details and reports relating to the phenomena of Satanic activity and demon-possession are to be studied, but they must be interpreted in the light of Scripture and not used to form a basis for conclusions or to colour the interpretation of Scripture.

Conclusions based on a series of 'case histories' and buttressed by selected Biblical texts derive from a method that has been used too often in recent popular books on Demonology and kindred themes and that must be repudiated. Some evangelicals who have written on Demonology have not paused to examine their method and have lost sight of the fact that 'the Supreme Judge, by which all controversies of religion are to be determined, and all decrees of councils, opinions of ancient writers, doctrines of men, and private spirits, are to be examined, and in whose sentence we are to rest, can be no other but the Holy Spirit speaking in the Scripture' (Westminster Confession of Faith, I, 10). Consequently they have been deceived by the claims of parapsychology in its many forms, including psychometry, clairvoyance and precognition. Thus we have seen Biblical prophecy discussed in terms of precognition ('second sight'). Jeremiah is alleged to have dictated part of his prophecy (Chap. 36) which he had received over a period of twenty years, and to have reproduced it when later destroyed, by means of psychometry (the use of some object for purposes of divination or recall). And the Judgment Day has been described in terms of retrocognition (the alleged ability to move backward in time). All this and much more like it has come from the pens of evangelical writers, resulting in a depressing and dangerous hotchpotch of Scripture, parapsychology and psychic research! This is not 'rightly handling the Word of Truth'. 'The infallible rule of interpretation of Scripture is the Scripture itself,' (Confession of Faith, I, 9), not Scripture read through the spectacles of Freud, Adler and Jung!

Dr Nevius has two valuable chapters dealing with the Biblical evidence, the rest of his book being devoted to an examination and refutation of other theories or explanations of the phenomena of demon-possession, such as the pathological and psychological theories, and to the consideration of a vast amount of testimony from missionaries in China, India, Japan and other areas. While the latter is interesting and necessary, it only serves to emphasize the need for a thorough study of this subject within the framework of Holy Scripture.

While we must try to evaluate the present resurgence of interest in demonic and occult phenomena, we need to remember that Satan's main efforts are in the field of belief and morals. This is the main battleground. And the adversary's hold on the unregenerate is in no way dependent on demonism and occultism, as these terms are popularly understood.

I am indebted to staff members of the Banner of Truth Trust for their help and guidance in the preparation of this work, in particular to Mr S. M. Houghton, and to my colleague, Prof. H. J. Blair, for his useful comments on certain Hebrew words. I am also grateful to Mrs V. Kelly, archivist in Aldersgate House, Belfast, for her willing assistance in checking sources relating to the time of the Wesleys, and for the facilities of the library of the Free Church College, Edinburgh.

F. S. L.

Kilraughts Reformed Presbyterian Church,
Co. Antrim,
July, 1975

1

ANGELS: GOOD AND EVIL

Any study of evil which fails to reckon with *the* Evil One must tend to become merely theoretical in its approach and fall short of the Biblical revelation on the subject. Even the spirit of this world, with its strife and turbulence, cannot be properly understood until there is an awareness of those spiritual forces which are as much opposed to man as they are to God. Christians who are virtually oblivious of the malignant opposition of the fallen angels, are to some extent deficient in caution and dependence upon God. Hence in the study of demonology we are not wasting time on the unimportant. The confrontation between God and Satan which centres on the cross of Christ is cosmic in its proportions and transcends the centuries of time. It is foolish and dangerous to wander, blind and deaf, along the firing line.

Before the subject of demonology can be seen in perspective there must be a knowledge of the Biblical doctrine of angels. Only then can there be profitable discussion of the nature, activity and judgment of Satan and his kingdom. Scripture throughout assumes the existence of angels and attributes personality to them. They have intelligence, moral character and all the essential expressions of personality. They are said to love, rejoice, desire, worship and converse. The Bible teems with such statements. The holy angels dwell with the redeemed in heaven and in certain respects the latter are said to resemble them (Matt. 22:30).

While on occasion angels have assumed bodily forms,

they are essentially spiritual beings. The writer to the Hebrews calls them 'ministering spirits', and their immaterial existence is implied in our Lord's statement that the redeemed in heaven 'neither marry, nor are given in marriage, but are as the angels of God' (Heb. 1:14; Matt 22:30). Spirits may be present in large numbers in one place at the same time. The Gadarene demoniac was called Legion 'because many demons were entered into him' (Luke 8:30). Abraham once saw what seemed to him a group of three men. One of the visitors immediately assumed control of the conversation and he is called Jehovah (Gen 18:1–15). Later the other two 'men' went towards Sodom, leaving Abraham alone with the Lord. We find them described as 'two angels' in the following chapter and thereafter they are referred to as 'men'. At the time of the resurrection of our Lord, the women who went to the sepulchre early in the morning saw an angel in the form of 'a young man' (Mark 16:5). We cannot say whether the bodies assumed by angels on such occasions were real or apparent. It is clear, however, that, while angels are much freer in relation to space and time than man, yet because they are created spirits they are finite. Their intelligence and power are obviously superhuman. They are said to 'excel in strength' (Psa 103:20). They are called Christ's 'mighty angels' (2 Thess 1:7). But the limitations of the angels are also indicated in Scripture. Speaking of the end of the age Christ said, 'But of that day and hour knoweth no man, no, not the angels of heaven, but my Father only' (Matt 24:36). We are, then, concerned with creatures which are solely spiritual, and are rational, moral and immortal. In the context of our present study the fact that they possess moral natures is important.

Angels Elect and Non-Elect:

The Scriptures speak of good and bad angels, of 'holy angels' and 'angels which kept not their first estate' (Jude 6). The angels are shown to be under moral obligation, being rewarded for obedience and punished for disobedience. The good angels are represented as forming the army or hosts of God, ever ready to obey His word. They 'do his commandments, hearkening unto the voice of his word' (Psa 103:20). The fallen angels form the army of Satan, the forces of darkness which endeavour to destroy the works of God. Christ describes the sowing of the tares among the wheat as the work of an enemy (Matt 13:28), and in the first Epistle of Peter Satan is called our 'adversary' (5:8). Both the holy angels and the fallen angels are great in number (Matt 26:53; Mark 5:9). We may say that angels constitute a company as distinguished from a race. Each was created separately and there is nothing in the angelic world corresponding to descent or procreation (Matt. 22:30). Consequently we may say that each apostate angel fell by himself, that is, by his own personal decision; whereas humanity, being a race, fell at once in its father and representative head.

The angels that did not sin are referred to in Scripture as the 'elect angels' (1 Tim 5:21). While all the angels collectively were holy by creation, and included in God's estimate of His creation as 'very good', some angels were the objects of a decree of election which preserved them from sinning. The non-elect angels were created holy, but were not, as the event proved, without the possibility of sinning. A consideration of 1 Tim 5:21 with its reference to the 'elect angels' and of 2 Pet 2:4 and Jude 6 which speak of 'the angels that sinned' and 'the angels which kept not their first estate', will show that angels as well as men are predestinated and foreordained, a realm in which it is dangerous to speculate. We are to confess what we believe because it has been revealed. Where there are gaps in the revelation, or in our understanding of the revelation, we must never try to fill them by a process of logic. It must suffice us to state that only a part of the angelic host was placed on probation, or created with the possibility of sinning, and that number did wilfully sin; whereas the perseverance of the elect angels was guaranteed by God's decree of election.

The elect angels needed no deliverance from sin (as do elect men) and so they are related to Christ as Head rather than as Mediator. They minister to Him and obey His commands (Matt 26:53). As to the divine decree relating to the angels that sinned, we are faced with a mystery. Here the curtain of revelation is closely drawn. For us the origin of evil is a baffling riddle. In this life at least it is the will of God that it should remain so. As W. G. T. Shedd reminds us, 'The certainty of sin by a permissive decree is an insoluble mystery for the finite mind'.[1] There is much in connection with the origin of sin which is veiled from our eyes, doubtless mercifully so.

Angelic Rank:

It is clear from Scripture that angels enjoy a measure of organization and rank. Different classes of angels are indicated. The word 'angel' simply means 'messenger' and designates one sent to men or sent by God. In Job 1:14 we read that a messenger came to Job. In the

1. *Dogmatic Theology*, Vol. 1, 420, Edinburgh 1889.

Septuagint[2] the word for angel is used. In Malachi 3:1, where God says 'Behold, I will send my messenger', the Septuagint reads 'angel'. In the New Testament the word is often applied to men. Christ, quoting the Old Testament, applies it to John the Baptist. God called him 'my messenger'.

More specifically the Scriptures speak of cherubim and seraphim. The cherubim are presented as guarding the entrance to paradise (Gen 3:24), looking upon the mercy-seat (Ex. 25:20), and as the chariot on which God descends to this earth (2 Sam 22:11; Psa 18:10). They are also spoken of as living beings in different forms (Ezek 1 and 10, Rev. 4). These symbolical representations serve to illustrate the power and dignity of such angels. The cherubim are intimately associated with the majesty and glory of God and are seen to declare His holiness in Eden, the tabernacle and the temple. Seraphim are mentioned in Isaiah 6. They also are symbolically represented in human form, with six wings, two covering the face, two the feet and two for swift obedience to God's word. In distinction from the cherubim they are represented as standing and serving before the throne of God, praising Him and ever waiting on His command.

There is Biblical reference to 'principalities', 'powers', 'thrones' and 'dominions' (Eph 3:10; Col 1:16, 2:10; Eph 1:21; 1 Pet 3:22). The terms indicate organization and rank. In most, possibly all, of the passages just listed the fallen angels are included, and in Ephesians 6:12 the 'principalities and powers' are definitely evil, being described as a fierce and deadly foe. We would by no means exclude the possibility of earthly powers being

2. A Greek translation of the Old Testament frequently quoted in the New Testament.

used as the instruments of these sinister forces on occasion, but it will not do to 'demythologize' these passages as Rudolph Bultmann and others have done, and explain them in terms of abstract 'demonism' and subliminal horrors which are beyond man's control. Not only is the Apostle Paul *not* demythologizing, he is emphasizing in the strongest possible manner the objective reality of depraved and hostile spirits. As E. K. Simpson puts it, Paul reminds Christ's soldiers 'that they are picked out to wrestle against principalities and powers supernaturally marshalled and not to be coped with except by virtue of supernatural aid'.[3]

Two of the holy angels are named in Scripture, Gabriel and Michael. Gabriel ('God's hero' or 'mighty one') is associated with the conveying and interpreting of divine revelations (Dan 8:16, 9:21; Luke 1:19.26), and is obviously an angel of considerable rank and importance. He hastens the realization of God's plans for the salvation of men. It is Gabriel who appears to Daniel to announce to him the return from the captivity and to focus his attention on the advent of the Messiah (Dan 8:16, 9:21), and it is he who, in the New Testament, announces to Zacharias the birth of John the Baptist (Luke 1:11–22) and to Mary the birth of the Saviour (Luke 1:19, 26). Frederic Godet terms him 'the heavenly evangelist'.[4] In an age of gloom and discouragement, when faith was severely tested, it is noteworthy that God sent an angel whose name bore witness to the might and energy of the Godhead. The appearance of such an angel on the field of

3. Comment on Ephesians 6:12, *New London Commentary*, Marshall, Morgan & Scott, 1957.

4. *Studies on the Old Testament*, 16, Hodder & Stoughton, 1874.

action was a pledge that nothing could frustrate God's gracious purpose.

Michael ('who is like unto God?') appears with even greater dignity and is called 'the archangel' (Jude 9). References to him in the Book of Daniel indicate that he is a 'prince' among the angels, and the expression 'one of the chief princes' (Dan 10:13) suggests ascending rank among angels, although such gradation does not necessarily imply a hierarchy of angels as is sometimes affirmed. It is interesting to note that Scripture does not speak of archangels, while theologians and commentators often do so. 'Archangel' occurs twice in the New Testament and in both instances it is used in the singular number, and once it is preceded by the definite article. The meaning of the name given to this mighty angel is significant. Placed at the very summit of the heavenly hosts, one thought apparently absorbs him, that of the immeasurable distance which separates him from the Creator. 'Who is like unto God?' As Godet puts it, 'at the very summit of all, he feels more than all others his own nothingness.'[5] Michael is seen as a valiant servant of Jehovah, fighting against the powers of evil,[6] the enemies of God and of His people.

The Employments of Angels:

The employments of the holy angels are rich and various. They are presented in Scripture as worshipping God (Matt 18:10), rejoicing in His works (Job 38:7),

5. Ibid., 15.
6. According to Luther, Hengstenberg and Patrick Fairbairn, Michael is another name for Christ and Calvin prefers this interpretation. Fairbairn argues at length in support of

executing His will (Psa 103:20), controlling as God's servants the affairs of nations (Dan 10:12, 13, 21; 11:1; 12:1), watching over the interests of particular churches (1 Tim 5:21, 1 Cor 11:10), assisting and protecting believers (1 Kings 19:5, Dan 6:22) and punishing God's enemies (Acts 12:23). There is no Biblical support for the idea that each Christian has his guardian angel, but there is evidence of something better than that. Each Christian enjoys the guardianship of angels as a whole (Heb 1:14). Matthew 18:10 has been cited in support of the former view. 'Their angels do always behold the face of my Father which is in heaven.' But the words do not necessitate the belief that every child of God has his own special angel. It seems wiser to interpret this passage in the light of the statement in Hebrews that believers enjoy a general ministry of angels.

At times angels are used in what has been termed 'extraordinary service', such as events in the lives of the patriarchs, the giving of the Law (Acts 7:53; Gal 3:19, Heb 2:2), and at the birth, resurrection and ascension of our Lord. At the second coming of Christ and the ensuing judgment they will again be prominent. While the angels do not administer God's regular providence, they

---

this view in his *Hermeneutical Manual*, 207ff., Edinburgh, 1858. And in Fairbairn's *Imperial Bible Dictionary* the same opinion is ably presented by George C. M. Douglas. One of the main difficulties with this view is the statement in Jude 9 that Michael, when contending with the devil, 'durst not bring against him a railing accusation, but said, The Lord rebuke thee.' It is by no means certain that the passages where Michael is named warrant the view that he is the second person of the Trinity. Edward J. Young, in his Commentary on Daniel, rejects the view that Michael is the Christ and supplies a convincing alternative interpretation.

may be regarded as ministers of His special providence in the life of the Church. Their intervention is occasional and exceptional, and only as they are expressly commanded by God. In no sense do angels come between us and God. Like the miracles, angelic appearances usually mark God's entrance upon fresh epochs and unfoldings of His redemptive purpose. We read of angels at the completion of creation, the giving of the Law, the birth of the Saviour, the temptation in the wilderness, the agony in Gethsemane, the resurrection, ascension and final judgment.

The evil angels also have their employments. They ceaselessly oppose God and strive to deflect His will. This is illustrated by the temptation of our first parents in Eden, the trials of Job and similar events. They are opposed to man's temporal and eternal welfare (Luke 13:11, 16; Acts 10:38; 2 Cor 12:7; 1 Thess 2:18). Yet they execute God's plans in spite of themselves (1 Kings 22:23; 1 Cor 5:5; 1 Tim 1:20). They owe allegiance to a high-ranking angel who sinned. Satan revolted against God and became the leader of all other rebel angels. Under his rule they are joined in a confederacy of evil and consequently we read of 'the devil and his angels' and 'the prince of demons'. He is given such names as Satan (adversary), Devil (slanderer), Apollyon (destroyer) and Belial (worthlessness or wickedness).[7] The Jews called him Beelzebub[8] and regarded him as Prince of the

7. See discussion of Belial in comment on 2 Cor 6:15 by P. E. Hughes, *New London Commentary*, Marshall, Morgan & Scott, 1962.

8. Most Biblical scholars regard the name as a contemptuous title, probably meaning 'dung-lord' or 'lord of the dung-hill', e.g., J. B. Lightfoot, J. A. Alexander, F. Godet, Albert Barnes.

demons. Satan is also termed the Dragon (a name associated with pagan powers in their opposition to the people of God, Ezek 29:3, Jer 51:34) and Serpent (Rev 20:2), a name which reminds us of his cunning. 'I fear', wrote the Apostle Paul, 'lest by any means, as the serpent beguiled Eve through his subtilty, so your minds should be corrupted from the simplicity that is in Christ' (2 Cor 11:3). The chief characteristics of the Evil One indicated by these various names are his power, malice, cunning and hostility.[9]

If we accept the Scriptures as the infallible Word of God then we are bound to accept their testimony concerning Satan, for as Charles Hodge reminds us, 'The rule of interpretation which gets rid of the doctrine of Satan and his influence, if carried out, would blot all the peculiar doctrines of the Scripture from the Bible. It has been so applied, to explain away the doctrines of sacrifice,

---

For other interpretations see Edersheim (*Life and Times of Jesus the Messiah*), *New Bible Dictionary* and J. N. Geldenhuys on Luke 11:15 (*New London Commentary*).

9. It is quite common to find the name Lucifer applied to the Devil. A literal translation of Isaiah 14:12 reads, 'How art thou fallen from the sky, thou star of light, sun of the dawn, hurled down to earth, thou that didst throw down nations from above!' The word translated 'star of light' derives from the Hebrew word 'to shine'. The idea is of the morning star, called in Latin, *lucifer*. In Isaiah 14 the word is applied to the king of Babylon (v.4), and the passage describes the fall of this arrogant ruler and his kingdom. In verses 13–15 we are shown the self-deification of this king, in which he was a type of antichrist (Dan 11: 36, 2 Thess 2:4). Some of the Church Fathers, such as Tertullian, regarded Luke 10:18 as an explanation of Isaiah 14:12, and so quite erroneously the name Lucifer was applied to the devil.

justification, heaven and hell.'[10] Once we tamper with any doctrine of Scripture, or seek to re-state it in what is glibly called 'modern thought-forms', there is no logical stopping-place short of a total rejection of the authority of the Bible as a divine revelation. 'Unbelief about the existence and personality of Satan', wrote J. C. Ryle, 'has often proved the first step to unbelief about God.'[11]

10. *Princeton Sermons*, No 59, Thomas Nelson & Sons, 1879.
11. *Expository Thoughts on the Gospels*, comments on Mark 5:1–17. James Clarke & Co., 1955.

2

SATAN'S PRESENT POSITION

Satan is represented in Scripture as the originator of evil, at least in the sense that he introduced it into our race. That is clear from the account of the Fall in Genesis 3, and from the words of our Lord in John 8:44: 'He was a murderer from the beginning and abode not in the truth, because there is no truth in him. When he speaketh a lie, he speaketh of his own: for he is a liar, and the father of it.' On this same occasion Christ declared to the scribes and Pharisees, 'Ye are of your father the devil, and the lusts of your father ye will do.' There is a definite link between the evil which is in Satan, and which consumes his whole being, and the evil which is in man. Hence he is called 'the prince of this world'.

The Scriptures also clearly view Satan as having a position of authority and leadership over the angelic hosts that shared in his revolt and expulsion from heaven. They alike share the spiritual depravity of their master. While some maintain that fallen angels are distinct from the demons, the former being imprisoned and enchained (Jude 6), it is generally agreed that such a distinction is not justified. The same titles are applied both to fallen angels and demons.

Paul hints at the sin which brought about the downfall of Satan. The man appointed to the office of bishop or overseer must not be a novice 'lest being lifted up with pride (Gk. inflated) he fall into the condemnation of the devil' (1 Tim. 3:6). The expression 'condemnation of the devil' in this passage means 'the condemnation pronounced upon the devil'. Satan's primal sin was essentially one of arrogance and pride. So it was with all the angels that sinned. They 'did not keep their own domain, but abandoned their proper abode'. (Jude 6). Their sin was that of arrogant revolt. The demons are in all respects like their master.

Satan and the demons are united in an alliance of evil. As J. J. Van Oosterzee remarks, 'It is not love alone which can join together – hate also can do it.'[1] Nor must we overlook the essential connection between this alliance and evil, for it is essentially an alliance of evil, and the true nature of sin is revealed in the Satanic revolt. 'The proper devilishness of sin is this', says Luther, 'that it *thus* modifies the first words of the Decalogue: I am *my* Lord and *my* God.'[2]

Satan is Bound:

In Scripture, then, we first meet Satan as a fallen creature and, by reason of sin, possessing a close relationship to both demons and our race. The extent of his influence among men we have also noted in the designation used by Christ, Satan is 'the prince of this world' (Jn 12:31, 14:30, 16:11). Similar terminology is to be found in the epistles. He is called 'the god of this world' and 'the prince of the power of the air'. Before there can be any satisfactory understanding of demonology it is essential for the right meaning to be given to these terms and titles.

Do they mean that Satan has received authority to rule over men? Is this world his dominion, prescribed to

1. *Christian Dogmatics*, 421, Hodder & Stoughton. 1881.
2. Ibid., 421.

him by God upon the fall of man? Was he therefore entitled to promise Christ all the kingdoms of the world? In modern Christian literature one frequently finds affirmative answers to these questions, indeed, the most staggering assertions are made respecting Satan's supposed dominion and power. Some speak of him as sovereign of this world, under a divine sentence which has not yet been executed. Or again, it is said that when Satan successfully tempted Adam he wrested the sceptre of authority from man and gained the right to rule the human race.[3] Certainly the Bible does not minimize the sinister power of the Evil One who is the prince of the demons and the head of a godless world-order, a power enhanced by the allegiance, witting or unwitting, of sinful men, and accommodated by the corruption of man's heart. But it remains to be asked if Satan is a monarch in some divinely granted domain, or a vanquished foe, an impostor, a liar and a deceiver.

Scripture leaves us in no doubt about the answer to this important question. Though Adam was a steward and trustee of God's creation, Satan had no authority to rule men, for man was never his own master. And therefore there could be no sceptre of rule belonging to man which was transferable to Satan after the Fall. God has given Satan no dominion over man. Man is within 'the dominion of Satan' (Acts 26:18) only because of his sin.[4] In revolt against God, he aligned himself with Satan. In this sense Satan is his 'god' and 'prince'; man is a captive in the jurisdiction of darkness (Col. 1:13).

3. See *Satan*, by Lewis Sperry Chafer, 13, The Sunday School Times Company, 1922.
4. See comment on Col 1:13 by F. F. Bruce, *New London Commentary*, Marshall, Morgan & Scott, 1957.

But the error with which we are now concerned appears much more clearly when Satan's relation to men is viewed in the light of the Lordship of Christ. Satan is not the present ruler of the world with Christ as the predicted future Lord. The binding of Satan does not belong to the 'not yet' of eschatology. By no means! The New Testament proclamation is that the sentence passed upon Satan in Eden *has* been executed! The truth about Satan is not merely that he is an unseated dignitary who was ejected from the courts of heaven; at the cross of Christ he has been crushed and routed upon earth! At Calvary Christ achieved total victory over Satan and his evil hosts. Of this truth the Scripture leaves us in no possible doubt. Jesus is said to have 'spoiled principalities and powers', and to have 'made a show of them openly, triumphing over them' in His cross (Col. 2:14, 15). He completely overcame the powers of evil. As F. F. Bruce remarks, He 'grappled with them and mastered them, stripping them of all the armour in which they trusted, and held them aloft in His mighty outstretched hands, displaying to the universe their helplessness and His own unvanquished strength.'[5] They were completely disabled at the cross where Christ stood before the whole moral universe as Victor Emmanuel. In no other way could we be delivered from the jurisdiction of darkness.

On the eve of His crucifixion Christ could say, 'Now is the judgment of this world: now shall the prince of this world be cast out' (Jn 12:32). The one whom this world served, and with whom it was allied, was to be *cast out* not in the remote future but 'now' – a word which is made emphatic in the Greek text by reason of its position in the sentence. Our Lord's statement is abundantly plain:

5. Comment on Col 2:15, *New London Commentary.*

through His death the expulsion of our chief enemy would become an accomplished fact. Satan's relation to men consists only in a common guilt and sinfulness; when the guilt of the redeemed is ended by the substitutionary sacrifice of Jesus their connection with Satan's domain must also end. This good news is bad news to the Evil One. It was bad news to him from the time of the first evangel of Genesis 3:15, 'And I will put enmity between thee and the woman, and between thy seed and her seed; it shall bruise thy head, and thou shalt bruise his heel'. Certainly we must not forget the efficacy of this gospel in Old Testament times, for the power of Calvary is retrospective as well as prospective in its effects (Rom. 3:25), yet it was with the accomplishment of Christ's sufferings that the completion of victory is announced. Immediately after Christ's statement that the prince of this world was cast out, He went on to say, 'And I, if I be lifted up from the earth will draw all men to myself' (John 12:32). The 'casting out' of Satan[6] is thus associated with the drawing of men from all parts of the world to Christ. Through Christ's cross God expels Satan from his domain in the hearts of men as soul after soul is translated 'into the kingdom of his dear Son'.

In harmony with Christ's words in John 12:32 is His statement that before the subjects of Satan are delivered the devil himself must be 'bound': 'No man can enter into a strong man's house, and spoil his goods, except he will first bind the strong man; and then he will spoil his house' (Mark 3:27). The establishment of Christ's kingdom required that Satan be first mastered and this we

6. It is significant that a word is used here which has the same root, in the original, as the term translated 'cast' into the abyss (A.V. 'bottomless pit'), Rev. 20:3.

find in the Gospels. We see Satan bound as our Lord triumphs over him in the temptation in the wilderness and as he casts out demons: 'If I with the finger of God cast out demons, no doubt the kingdom of God is come upon you' (Luke 11:20). Again, when the seventy missionaries reported, 'Lord, even the demons are subject to us through thy name,' He observed, 'I beheld Satan falling as lightning from heaven' (Luke 10:17, 18).

The 'binding' of Satan through Christ is a constantly emerging motif in the New Testament. Satan is 'judged', 'spoiled' and 'destroyed' (Heb. 2:14). It is significant to note that the same word for binding which is used in Matthew 12:29, where Christ speaks of binding the strong man, is again applied to Satan in Revelation 20. We take the 'thousand years' of that chapter to refer to the whole of the New Testament dispensation, the dispensation in which we live, and the binding there spoken of took place with the first coming of the Lord Jesus Christ.[7] His power was curbed so that he could no longer deceive the nations with the measure of success that he once was permitted to enjoy. He would be unable to hinder the spread of the Gospel throughout the earth and in this sense would 'deceive the nations no more'. This is not to say that God would not allow Satan to 'hinder' His servants at different times in the history of the Church, but simply to affirm the plain truth of Scripture that Satan cannot prevent the spread of the Gospel in the earth or

7. Space and the nature of this study forbid our giving reasons for this conviction, but for such reasons the reader is referred to William Hendriksen's commentary on the book of Revelation, *More than Conquerors* (Baker Book House, 1956), and Oswald T. Allis' *Prophecy and the Church* (The Presbyterian and Reformed Publishing Company, 1945).

thwart God's sovereign purpose for His Church and for the world.[8] As Hendriksen well says, 'We conclude that also here in Rev 20:1-3 the binding of Satan and the fact that he is hurled into the abyss to remain there for a thousand years indicates that throughout this present Gospel Age, which begins with Christ's first coming and extends nearly to the second coming, the devil's influence on earth is curtailed so that he is unable to prevent the extension of the Church among the nations by means of an active missionary programme. During this entire period he is prevented from causing the nations – the world in general – to destroy the Church as a mighty, missionary institution.'[9]

Is the Lion Really Chained?:

To many people, including not a few Christians, the statement that Satan is even now cast out sounds hollow and unreal. He does not seem to be cast out. Those who live in areas where terrorism is rife and who are almost daily confronted by the appalling results of man's in-humanity to man, often find it difficult to believe that at Calvary Satan was routed. 'God is sovereign', said a minister in Northern Ireland recently, to which he received the reply from a member of his congregation, 'He doesn't seem to be sovereign'.

In regard to this problem there are several things which must be said. We must understand that the Bible does not teach that the binding of Satan eliminates wickedness from the earth or renders Satan and his

8. For a discussion of 'Satan hindered us' (1 Thess 2:18) see p. 49.
9. Ibid., 226ff.

minions immobile. In Jude 6 we read that the fallen angels are enchained for ever, yet these demons are far from inactive as the Gospels testify. Satan is one of those enchained angels, but this in no way implies a complete cessation of activity on his part. In Bunyan's *Pilgrim's Progress*, Christian was afraid when he saw two lions in the way. It was this same sight which had made Mistrust and Timorous turn back. 'The lions were chained', wrote Bunyan, 'but he saw not the chains.' Satan and the demons are cast into the abyss (variously translated 'bottomless pit', 'deep' and 'pit' in the New Testament). The demons who possessed the Gadarene maniac besought our Lord that He would not cast them into the abyss (Luke 8:31). Although the abyss was their proper habitation, yet under the permissive will of God and for His own purposes they are allowed a certain activity on the earth until that day when they will be confined to the abyss for ever.

It must also be understood that while God will crush Satan under our feet because of Christ's total victory, the two events are not co-incident in point of time. 'The God of peace shall bruise Satan under your feet *shortly* (or speedily)' is the glorious promise of the victorious outcome of *our battle* with Satan. As Robert Haldane puts it, 'There were two victories to be obtained over Satan. By the first, his head was to be bruised under the feet of Jesus Christ; and by the second, the rest of his body will be bruised under the feet of believers.'[10] The second victory will be as complete as the first!

Of course, it is only from the standpoint of the finite creature that there seems to be a gap between the victory

10. *Exposition of the Epistle to the Romans* (16:20), The Banner of Truth Trust, 1958.

of Christ over Satan and the final disposal of the defeated foe in the victory of the Church. To human eyes the victory of Calvary seems almost unreal in view of the tragedy and turmoil of our modern world. Frequently the illustration of sentence passed and judgment yet to be executed is used. But this does not agree with Scripture, which, as we have seen, tells us very plainly that the sentence passed in Eden was executed at Calvary. A better illustration would be that of thunder and lightning. In objective reality these are virtually one, but from our standpoint, owing to the fact that light travels much more quickly than sound, there is usually a time-lag between seeing the flash and hearing the thunder. With God the victory and the judgment are all in the cross. '*Now* shall the prince of this world be cast out' (Jn 12:31). 'The prince of this world is judged'. (Jn 16:11). But to the believer who lives in time, there is a time-lag between the lightning and the thunder, between Satan being cast down and the hearing of the crash of his fall. With God there is no such gap and at the final judgment, when time will have ended, we shall see for ourselves that the cross stood at the heart of history and that there Satan was in fact cast out.

The Christian Attitude to Satan:

As we shall observe in a subsequent chapter it is a dangerous thing to regard Satan as of little or no consequence. He is still a vicious enemy, a tempter, and 'a roaring lion'. But our present concern is to demonstrate how it is no less perilous to hold exaggerated views of Satan's authority and power. The conflict between God and Satan is not a struggle between two great powers with the outcome in the balance. We fight a mortally wounded foe! Satan's counter-offensive is as hopeless as it is fierce. We must not believe his proud claim to the 'kingdoms of the world'; His pretension to dominion is a lie. He is a usurper with no authority. It is God who holds the world in His hand, not this arch-pretender. And in God's world Satan is an impostor, a squatter with no rights. Robert Recker is so right when he says, 'To succumb to acknowledging Satan's right to rule would be treason to Christ; it is an expression of unbelief, and at worst of idolatry.'[11] As Christians we are summoned to confess *here and now* that 'Jesus Christ is Lord, to the glory of God the Father'. It is because we have a regnant Saviour that we are, in His strength, to 'resist the devil' and he will flee from us. (Jas 4:7). With the shield of faith we shall be able to quench all the fiery darts of the wicked one, and strong in the Lord and in the power of His might, and clad in the whole armour of God, we shall be able to stand against the wiles of the devil.

The binding of Satan is so real that he has no authority or power over the Christian. In Christ the believer is safe and victorious. The 'wicked one toucheth him not' (1 Jn 5:18). As the prince of darkness, on our Lord's own testimony, has no authority over Him (Jn 14:30) so he has none over those who are in Christ and who share in His victory over evil. Our Saviour is victorious! He is the Lion of the tribe of Judah (Gen 49:9, Rev 5:5). He divides the spoil with the strong (Isa 53:12). The child born at Bethlehem is 'the Mighty God' (Isa 9:6). The Lamb of God who went to the sacrifice, now goes forth 'conquering and to conquer' (Rev 6:2).

11. *Satan: In Power or Dethroned?* Calvin Theological Journal, Vol 6, No 2.

The Christian cannot rightly view his adversary unless the triumph of Christ is given its proper place. If our faith does not see Christ as all-victorious, we shall know little of victory. Even in the face of demonic power the Christian is to rejoice in the words of Paul, 'But thanks be unto God who always leadeth us in triumph' (2 Cor 2:14).

3

THE STRATEGY OF THE ENEMY

As we have seen, Satan appears in Eden as deposed from the position he once held in heaven and expelled from the immediate presence of God. He has neither right nor title, and there is not the slightest indication that he acquired any rights in Eden. On the contrary he was *cursed* of God. This was the ultimate thrust of the punishment of the serpent, which creature was merely the instrument of the Evil One. In Genesis 3 we see that Satan is completely within God's power and there is no hint of Satan having any right to the sinner or any legal dominion. Nowhere in Scripture is Satan presented as victorious. This is not to deny his malice and power. The Scriptures provide evidence of both. Yet from the outset we observe Satan as wholly arrogant. He offers man an alien wisdom in place of the wisdom of God. He openly contradicts the word of God, or, if it suits him better, twists and distorts it. He is a thorough-going rationalist, submitting the laws of God to the judgment of the creature's reason. He cynically seeks to repudiate the genuineness of the righteous man's faith. He makes grandiose claims which are completely fictitious. He is the 'father of lies'. And behind this fabrication of sophistry and pretension, he wages constant warfare against God, His creation and His Church.

Satan the Clever Foe:

In Genesis 3 the devil appears as 'most clever' (A.V. 'more subtle'). He does not openly attack Eve, but insidiously casts a doubt on the word of God to her. Is it really the case that God has said, 'Ye shall not eat from every tree of the garden'? The question seems to suggest that God is putting an unwelcome and unfair restriction upon man. Satan ignores the fact that man may make full use of all other trees in the garden. There is an abundance and a variety which more than meet human requirements. Instead he singles out the one tree of which man may not eat and remarks with feigned astonishment and indignation, 'Surely not!' Suspicion is cast upon God's goodness. For Eve to harbour such suspicion for one moment, in view of God's love and gracious provision, would be *sin*. It would mean that she no longer believed God and no longer trusted Him. Having questioned the word of God, Satan proceeds to deny it and virtually to call God a liar. 'Ye shall not surely die!' Then he attacks God's motive in forbidding man to eat of this tree. 'God doth know that in the day ye eat thereof, then your eyes shall be opened, and ye shall be as gods, knowing good and evil.' Beneath the subtle, rationalistic approach of the Evil One there lies the most blasphemous denial of the goodness and righteousness of God. And furthermore he sets up his own 'goodness' against that of God, calling in question the divine love and faithfulness. As to justice, he professes to be more righteous than the Almighty. He would dare sit in judgment on the Judge of all the earth. Here we see the utmost presumption and profanity parading in the guise of the most unselfish philanthropy. The prince of darkness appears as an angel of light. The diabolical cunning of the temptation lies in its apparent offer of something good – 'Ye shall be as gods.'

The tempter came to Adam and Eve with cynical composure and questioned their whole covenant relationship with God, casting doubt on the veracity of His word to them and posing as their friend and benefactor. Eve detected no animosity in the one who claimed to speak in the name of truth. But when our first parents accepted the Satanic alternative to the divine covenant, they entered another 'world', 'this present evil world', as it is called in the New Testament, and became subject to Satan and his lie. Instead of faith in divine revelation, man now asserted the sufficiency of human reason to interpret all things. Man became, in his own estimation, the reference point of all meaning. In place of his creaturehood, he acclaimed his own autonomy and, in his own eyes, became 'master of his fate' and 'captain of his soul'. From a sovereign God who plans and requests all things, man now turned to a vaunted self-determination, whereas in actual fact Satan was leading him captive at his will. The presuppositions of modern thought were introduced into Eden by Satan and freely accepted by Adam and Eve. They are basic to all the tempter said to Eve and are intrinsic in man's sin.

Thus man became a rebel against God. He joined forces with Satan. The fall was no mere act of stumbling, but a catastrophe of the first magnitude. In a moment of time man passed from life to death. And Satan has never dropped the swaggering approach with which he challenged God in Eden. His arrogance and lies persist unabated. It is profitable to read the Bible with an eye on Satan's claims and poses, and God's dealings with him.

Satan Asking for a Soul:

Satan's approach to God, as described in the book of Job, bears all the marks of his usual defiant cynicism. Yet it is plain that he can only act against Job as God permits him. H. L. Ellison points out that 'Satan cannot even mention Job until God invites him to do so' (1:8; 2:3), and adds, 'Equally he has no power over Job or his possessions until God gives it to him . . . He is not sovereign in a rival kingdom, but a rebel to whom God gives as much rope as will glorify His name.'[1] Satan fills a subservient role in the story of Job. Having stripped Job of earthly wealth and comfort, he is cast aside as of no further interest, and is not even mentioned at the close of the story. One lesson that we learn from Job, among many more, is that all power and authority belong to God. There is no dualism here.

It is interesting to compare the case of Job with that of Peter and the other apostles as described in Luke 22:31. Christ said to Peter, 'Simon, Simon, behold, Satan hath desired to have you, that he may sift you as wheat.' Literally this reads, 'Satan obtained you by asking.' This implies that his request was granted. Judas, into whom Satan had entered, had just departed on his dark mission. Judas was chaff. Satan would sift *all* the apostles as wheat is sifted. Apparently the accusation is the same as in the case of Job. Satan would seek to prove each of them a Judas – chaff! That Satan's request was not limited to Peter is indicated by the plural 'you'. Satan was permitted to try them all. (Matt 26:31, 56; Mark 14:27, 50). And Christ prayed for them all, with the exception of Judas

1. *From Tragedy to Triumph*, 25, The Paternoster Press, 1958.

(Jn 17). Yet Luke 22:32 shows that Christ prayed particularly for Peter that his faith might not fail utterly, but that in due course he might strengthen his brethren. So in the winnowing of the Twelve, the ultimate contest was between Christ and Satan, and Satan could only subject the apostles to this severe test by express permission of God. And as in the case of Job, the regenerate, by the grace of God, stood the test. Judas alone was chaff. Satan's accusations were proved false.

The Accuser of the Brethren:

In the third chapter of Zechariah we read of Satan's opposition to the Church of God, for Joshua the high priest in this passage personifies and represents Israel. He prays for all the people, symbolically bears the nation's guilt and on its behalf enters into the most holy place. 'So *his* condition is *Israel*'s condition, *his* acquittal a typical way of expressing *theirs*; the words of comfort and assurance given to *him* apply with equal validity to *them*.'[2] Satan appears in this passage as the *adversary* of the high priest,[3] and his charges against him and consequently against God's people, are answered by Jehovah Himself (v.2f.,), because it is *His* servant who has been attacked. We are at once reminded of Revelation 12:10, '. . . the accuser of our brethren is cast down, which accused them before our God day and night.' It is quite clear from the opening chapters of Job and from Zechariah 3, and indeed from Genesis 3:14, that there is,

2. *Exposition of Zechariah*, 64, H. C. Leupold, Baker Book House, 1965.
3. 'Satan' means adversary and 'to resist him' (Jas 4:7) is literally 'to be his adversary'!

at times, a certain communication between God and Satan, and that Satan is granted a certain limited intelligence of God's will, purpose and power. Later we shall see this further illustrated in the New Testament by certain recorded utterances of demons.

The Scriptures also indicate that believers may unwittingly become Satan's tools. In 1 Chronicles 21:1 we are told that Satan incited David to number Israel, and from 2 Samuel 24:1 we may infer that even this influence could only be exerted by divine permission. The same satanic influence upon believers is indicated in the New Testament where we read that Peter at one point became the mouthpiece of Satan and was addressed as such by our Lord.

Satan Tempting our Lord:

God cannot be tempted with evil (Jas 1:13). The temptation of our Lord in the wilderness (Matt 4:1–11; Mark 1:12, 13; Luke 4:1–13) was addressed to Him in His human nature. It is noteworthy that this· trial followed soon after the baptism of Christ. In His baptism He was fully equipped by the Holy Spirit for His public ministry and His appearance as the Messiah. Once the prophet Isaiah cried, 'Oh that thou wouldest rend the heavens, that thou wouldest come down!' Mark records, 'And straightway coming up out of the water, he saw the heavens opened (Gk rent, or cloven), and the Spirit like a dove descending upon him' (1:10). This was an answer to Isaiah's cry, and to the prayers of generations of believers. Christ stood that day as the sinner's substitute and representative; He stood completely under the law, the law to which He had been subject in His circumcision and presentation in the temple. And so He insisted that John baptize him. 'Suffer it to be so now: for thus it become thus to fulfil all righteousness' (Matt 3:15). On this occasion God the Father owned Christ as His only-begotten Son in the most absolute sense. By His Spirit He gave Him that armour with which He would defeat the power of darkness. Christ immediately went forth to use it and in this action He was impelled (Mark has 'driven') by the Holy Spirit. A literal translation of Luke's introduction to the Temptation reads, 'And Jesus, full of the Holy Spirit, returned from Jordan, and was led *in* the Spirit *in* the wilderness during forty days, being tempted of the devil.' In other words He was not merely led to the wilderness, but guided throughout His struggle there by the Spirit, equipped with His fulness and in the enjoyment of unbroken fellowship with the Father. Thus He freely, actively and gloriously won the battle.

In some respects the temptation of Christ is the counterpart of that of Adam and Eve. The battle was about to be won on the same ground of humanity on which previously it had been lost. The 'last Adam' would meet the tempter's wiles and reject them one by one. He faced the same old enemy using the same technique that he used in Eden. True, he did not come in disguise, but otherwise the assault has certain features in common with that in Eden. In both temptations the issues are crucial. The first representative of our race failed the test and man fell. Now all is again at issue. The second Adam represents His people and Satan uses all his guile and cunning in the attack. This is not to equate the temptation of Christ with that of Adam, as if it were a mere repetition. As we shall see, the temptation of the Messiah is unique.

In approaching Adam and Eve in the garden, Satan faced the unknown. Would Adam disobey? Could he be persuaded to sin? The outcome of that temptation was unknown to the tempter. Now, in the case of the 'last Adam' Satan again faced the unknown. The incarnation presented him with an entirely new situation. This was not only Christ incarnate, but Christ in a state of humiliation, coming as a servant and subject to the law. Could he break His Messiahship at this point? Could he destroy His Messianic status? Could he lead the Messiah into sin? He had anticipated the incarnation and had done his utmost to prevent it and so nullify what he had heard from God in Eden. He repeatedly sought to destroy the chosen race, to wipe out the royal seed, and at the incarnation itself his mailed fist was raised to strike down the holy Child. From that moment onwards the onslaught had been intensified and he returned again and again to the attack. Later, our Lord was to refer to his 'temptations' (Luke 22:28). What is commonly termed 'the temptation' occurred at the end of a contest lasting forty days, a struggle which was physically exhausting to the Saviour. When the forty days were ended 'he . . . hungered'. But there is more than the hunger of a prolonged fast indicated here, for both Matthew and Mark record that when Satan finally withdrew, angels ministered unto our Lord. We may compare the conflict in Gethsemane when 'there appeared an angel unto him from heaven, strengthening him' (Luke 22:43). It was at the end of a lengthy period of temptation that Satan made his desperate attempt to break the Messianic loyalty and integrity of Jesus and so lead Him to sin.

The first temptation is to be seen as a suggestion selfishly to exploit His power to meet His own need by turning stones into bread. The second temptation was a call to give a grand display of Messiahship so that He might be acknowledged as the Christ at once; and the third temptation an attempt to make Christ accept the political and nationalistic conception of Messiahship.

The first two temptations are plainly connected with our Lord's Messianic calling which involved Him in humiliation as the suffering Servant. They are introduced by the phrase, 'If thou be the Son of God.' In the original Greek this expression is non-committal.[4] It does not necessarily imply doubt, although it was probably intended to give rise to doubt in Jesus: 'Has God said, Thou art my beloved Son, and yet forbidden Thee to give Thyself bread?' The third temptation was not patently connected with Christ's Messianic task, but then we would not expect Christ's divine Sonship and Satan-worship to be mentioned in the same breath by the enemy. Had the third temptation succeeded it would have destroyed Christ's Messianic work, and so we may regard this threefold attack as being aimed at the Messianic status of Jesus Christ. In each case 'that old serpent' was foiled. All his subterfuge had failed. Summarily dismissed by Christ, he withdrew 'for a season'.

'For a season' suggests a return to the attack, and in the Gospels we can trace some of those fresh assaults. Christ was not addressing Peter so much as the Evil One himself, when He said in words reminiscent of the temptation in the wilderness, 'Get thee behind me, Satan' (Matt 16:23). Peter undoubtedly was rebuked, but the

4. See W. F. Arndt, *Commentary on Luke*, 130, Concordia Publishing House, 1956; and A. Plummer, *Commentary on Luke*, 109, T & T Clark, 1896.

strength of the rebuke was called forth by Christ's awareness of Satan's stealthy approach. In the garden of Gethsemane Christ was again conscious of a renewed onslaught which would reach its height at Calvary. Shortly before the agony in the garden Christ declared, 'The prince of this world cometh, and hath nothing in me' (Jn 14:30). At His arrest He said, 'This is your hour, and the power of darkness' (Luke 22:53). He saw clearly that Satan was behind the unholy plots of His oppressors.

In the threefold attack at the end of the protracted struggle in the wilderness, Satan showed remarkable shrewdness and a profound insight into the real issues at stake. Christ's answers, when studied in their Old Testament context, clearly indicate that Satan was not merely trying to lead Christ to sin, but was seeking to conquer Him at the crucial point on which His whole work of redemption depended. He was endeavouring to move Christ out of the spirit of humiliation in which He now stood and away from the pathway of suffering which He had set His face to follow. What would have been quite appropriate for Him in His subsequent exaltation would have been wrong now. The enemy was trying to persuade Him to take a short-cut to His Messianic glory and so to by-pass the dark night of suffering and sorrow. This is the real animus of the Temptation. Satan knew that if he could only break Christ's adherence to the principle of humiliation, he would have wrecked the whole plan of redemption. But his failure to deflect Christ from the way that God had called Him to follow was absolute. Christ emerged from the fray unscathed and triumphant. He knew well the real nature of Satan's attack and it is noteworthy that He who was 'made under the law, to redeem them that were under the law' (Gal 4:4, 5), replied to each of Satan's suggestions with a quotation from Deuteronomy, the Book of the Law. Christ refused to abandon the *via dolorosa*, or break His oath-bound covenant with the Father. Always He could say, as He went to His cross, 'My meat is to do the will of him that sent me, and to finish his work' (John 4:34).

The temptation of the Son of God by the Devil was thorough and exhaustive. Satan struck with all the skill at his disposal at the very heart of Christ's Messianic calling; he subjected Him to the utmost heat of seduction, but the Holy One of God never wavered. He emerged from temptation's fire as pure gold. What else would we expect of incarnate Deity?

Satan's Boast of World Dominion:

Nowhere is Satan's swaggering pretension more apparent than in his boast of world dominion and his professed ability to give it to Christ. Calvin calls it an 'imposture'.[5] Our Lord knew that Satan was a usurper, arrogating powers to himself which he did not possess. Satan's claim to have dominion over 'the kingdoms of the world' is a lie. It is God, not the arch-pretender, who holds the world in His hand. And in God's world Satan is a lying impostor, a squatter without rights. The dispensationalist writer, Lewis Sperry Chafer, rejects the view that Satan's claim was false and does so on two grounds. The offer, he suggests, would have had no value had Satan not possessed what he offered; and a 'false claim would have been immediately branded as a lie by the

5. Comment on Luke 4:6.

Son of God'.[6] However if Christ had worshipped Satan the false offer would have had 'value' from the standpoint of the tempter and the fact that our Lord brushed Satan's temptation aside by insisting that God alone must be worshipped does not mean that He placed any credence on Satan's proud claim. Geldenhuys comments on Luke 4:5–8; 'In these words Satan appears in his true colours, as the arch-deceiver and the aspirant after the power and glory which belong only to God. It is, indeed, true that by God's permission the kingdoms of the world (in so far as sin rules in the hearts and lives of the leaders and also of the individual members of the nations) have been delivered to him. Thus Jesus Himself spoke of him as the prince of this world. But He did not mean it in an absolute sense as the arch-deceiver himself pretended. Only to the extent that mankind surrender themselves in sin to the evil one does God permit him to rule over the world of men, but nevertheless always under His highest and final overruling, so that everything in the end leads to His glory. God never lets the reins slip out of His hands.'[7]

The Scriptures throughout insist on the absolute and undiminished sovereignty of God over this earth, as for instance in the twenty-fourth Psalm: 'The earth is the Lord's, and the fulness thereof; the world, and they that dwell therein.' The Old Testament, as much as the New, presents us with a picture of Satan as one whose power is always subject to divine permission. He is neither omnipotent, omniscient nor omnipresent. In vain do we search the Old Testament for Satan reigning over God's world.

6. Ibid., 53.
7. *Commentary on the Gospel of Luke*, 160. Marshall, Morgan & Scott, 1950.

What are the kingdoms and rulers of this world, Satan and his legions included, as compared with the sovereign Ruler of the universe? His own word is impressively clear. 'Behold, the nations are as a drop of a bucket, and are counted as the small dust of the balance: ... all nations before him are as nothing; and they are counted to him less than nothing, and vanity' (Isa 40:15, 17). God 'is a great King over all the earth' (Psa 47:2). The prophecy of Isaiah is particularly impressive in this respect. In chapter 45 we are confronted with the divine declaration, 'I am the LORD, and there is none else, there is no God beside me.' Nine times in this single chapter God says that 'there is none else' or 'no God beside me'. So much for Satan's pretensions to sovereignty!

Christ the King:

Is Satan a reigning foe, or has he been vanquished at the cross? The Bible consistently presents him as crushed and defeated. Yet as we live and move in the sequence of time he is still dangerous even in his death throes. Our Saviour is 'a great King over all the earth' (Psa 47:2). His dominion is universal (Psa 72). He is 'Governor among the nations' (Psa 22:28), 'higher than the kings of the earth' (Psa 89:27), 'King of nations' (Jer 10:6, 7), 'the Prince of the kings of the earth' (Rev 1:5) and 'King of kings, and Lord of lords' (Rev 19:16). This is the mediatorial reign of Christ, for to Him the Father has given all power or authority in heaven and in earth (Matt 28:18). 'And there was given Him dominion, and glory, and a kingdom, that all people, nations, and languages, should serve Him: His dominion is an everlasting dominion, which shall not pass away, and His kingdom that which shall not be destroyed' (Dan 7:14). To acknowledge Satan's right to rule in any sphere whatsoever is treason to the Christ of God and an expression of unbelief.

4

OUR ADVERSARY THE DEVIL

While there is the danger of holding exaggerated views of Satan's authority and power, it is just as dangerous to regard him as of little or no consequence. It is quite clear from Scripture that the 'binding' of Satan refers to his inability to act without the permissive will of God, but in so far as he acts at all he is a vicious enemy and we are frequently warned in Scripture to be watchful and ready for his attacks. We read of his 'fiery darts' (Eph 6:16) and we are urged to be sober and vigilant, because our 'adversary the devil, as a roaring lion, walketh about, seeking whom he may devour; whom resist steadfast in the faith . . .' (1 Pet 5:8, 9). 'Neither give place to the devil', writes Paul (Eph 4:27). 'Resist the devil and he will flee from you', declares James (4:7). Paul writes to Timothy about 'the snare of the devil' (1 Tim 3:7; cf., 2 Tim 2:26). Our warfare against the forces of darkness is so intense that it is imperative that we be clad from head to foot in 'the whole armour of God' (Eph 6:11–17).

We must strike a Scriptural balance between the truth that Satan is a crushed, defeated foe, and the truth that he is on the prowl like a hungry lion. In other words, we must avoid the extreme of regarding him as a reigning foe, and the extreme, equally wrong, of not taking him seriously. Both extremes are condemned by Scripture. We are given abundant evidence in the New Testament of the continuing malevolent activity of Satan in human affairs. Frequently this activity is of such a nature that its satanic source is not suspected by man.

Satan's Use of Physical Forces:

In Luke 13:16 we read of a devout woman, described by our Lord as 'a daughter of Abraham' and attending the place of worship, yet suffering from 'a spirit of infirmity', that is, a spirit causing infirmity.[1] Professor A. Rendle Short was of the opinion that she suffered from the disease *spondylitis deformans* in which 'the bones of her spine were fused into a rigid mass'.[2] Luke says that she was 'bowed together, and could in no wise lift up herself'.[3] Christ said that she was one 'whom Satan had bound, lo, these eighteen years'. Her physical affliction was Satanic in origin but the term 'daughter of Abraham' precludes the notion that she is to be regarded as a particularly wicked or immoral person. It will not do to argue that she was imprisoned by a wrong mental attitude to her affliction and that it was this attitude which was of evil origin. The whole passage clearly indicates that our Lord referred her physical condition to the malice of Satan. While not demon-possessed, her suffering had been imposed on her by an evil spirit. The healing of this woman by our Lord was part of a ministry which included 'healing all that were oppressed of the devil' (Acts 10:38).

The apostle Paul experienced 'a thorn in the flesh, the messenger of Satan to buffet me, lest I should be exalted

1. See J. N. Geldenhuys' *Commentary on the Gospel of Luke*, Marshall, Morgan & Scott, 1961.
2. *Modern Discovery and the Bible*, 127, Inter-Varsity Fellowship, 1961.
3. For the medical use of terms employed in this passage by the physician Luke, see *The Medical Language of St. Luke*, W. K. Hobart, Dublin, 1882, and republished by Baker Book House, 1954.

above measure' (2 Cor 12:7). Whatever the nature of
this 'thorn', its origin must not be overlooked.[4] The
apostle was fully conscious of Satan's opposition to his
life's work. 'Wherefore', he writes, 'we would have
come unto you, even I Paul, once and again; but
Satan hindered us' (1 Thess 2:18). The word translated
'hindered' is a strong word and means 'to cut into'.
Commenting on this same word in Galatians 5:7,
Lightfoot describes it as 'a metaphor derived from
military operations'. The word signifies 'to break up a
road' (by destroying bridges etc.) so as to render it
impassable . . .[5] While the reference in 1 Thessalonians
2:18 to Satan's strong opposition does not specifically
refer to any physical visitation, it could, in the light of
2 Corinthians 12:7, include such an affliction on certain
occasions.

In 1 Corinthians 5 Paul discusses a peculiarly offensive
form of sexual immorality which had occurred in the
Corinthian church. Exercising his full apostolic authority,
he decides to deliver this man 'unto Satan for the
destruction of the flesh, that the spirit may be saved in
the day of the Lord Jesus'. Many commentators take the
view that 'flesh' in this passage means 'sinful flesh', and
that this deliverance unto Satan aims at the destruction of
the sinner's sinful nature. When it is urged that Satan
would not and could not destroy sin, the exponents of this
view reply that the passage does not state that Satan
destroys the sin, but that the deliverance unto Satan has
this destruction as a result, and 2 Corinthains 12:7 is

4. See Philip E. Hughes on 'Paul's Thorn in the Flesh',
Commentary on 2 Corinthians, *New London Commentary*,
Marshall, Morgan & Scott, 1962.

5. *Galatians*, J. B. Lightfoot, Macmillan & Co., 1921.

quoted in support of this idea.[6] Paul's thorn in the flesh was 'the messenger of Satan' to buffet him, lest he should be 'exalted above measure'. But this interpretation of 1 Corinthians 5:1–5 overlooks the important fact that when, in the New Testament, *flesh* stands opposed to *spirit*, it means the physical body.[7] And in the passage in question this understanding of the word 'flesh' is reinforced by the fact that the man to be delivered to Satan was guilty of a sin of the flesh (body). He was to be punished for licentiousness of life. The word translated 'destruction' is strong and implies physical suffering. The punishment would relate to the nature of the offence. Satan would be permitted by God to 'destroy' the body that the soul might be saved, God using this ordeal to lead the sinner to repentance. And so the man was delivered to the power of Satan 'in the name of our Lord Jesus Christ', 'with the power of our Lord Jesus Christ', and with a view to the man's salvation 'in the day of the Lord Jesus'. Thus it becomes evident that Satan had the power to afflict the man's body, but could only do so as permitted by God.[8] Since apostolic times, the Church has often witnessed this same principle at work. The Christian pastor has occasionally witnessed the severe affliction of the body, and at times its near destruction, before the soul was saved.

6. See F. W. Grosheide, Commentary on 1 Corinthians, *New London Commentary*, Marshall, Morgan & Scott, 1954.

7. This point is well made by Charles Hodge in his Commentary on 1 Corinthians. Compare the comments of Albert Barnes, Calvin, Leon Morris, Robertson and Plummer (*International Critical Commentary*) on this passage.

8. With reference to the power of the apostles to inflict physical punishment, it is interesting to compare Acts 5:1–11; 13:9–11; 2 Cor. 10:8 and 13:10.

This same power of Satan can also relate in a malevolent fashion to the forces of nature. Not only did Satan smite Job 'with sore boils from the sole of his foot unto his crown' (Job 2:7), he turned the lightning flash against his flocks and servants (1:16) and sent a howling gale which destroyed the house where Job's sons and daughters were eating, and all perished save one servant (v.19). Joseph Caryl, the seventeenth-century divine, in his classic Commentary on the Book of Job, remarks, 'The Lord Who holdeth the wind in His fists gave Satan power, and he brought a terrible wind.' Caryl adds, 'When we consider the power and policy of Satan, let us bless God that he cannot stir to do us that mischief which his nature at once inclines and enables him to do, until God permits him'.[9] But once granted this permission, Satan can and does employ the forces of nature in an abortive attempt to frustrate God's purpose and discredit His people.

It may be significant in the account of Christ's stilling of the tempest, recorded in Matthew, Mark and Luke, that He 'rebuked' the winds and the sea. All three Evangelists use the same term. In Mark's account there are the additional words, 'Peace, be still'; literally, 'be muzzled'. Since the storm is addressed as if it were a rational agent, it is hard to consider this form of address without recognizing the probability that Christ was addressing the one who is the ultimate ground of all disharmony in nature and whose tireless hatred was expressed in a storm which threatened the occupants of that small boat. This seems all the more likely when we remember that Christ 'rebuked' a demon, saying, 'Hold thy peace', or, 'Be muzzled'. The view that the storm on

9. *Exposition of Job*, 6, Sovereign Grace Publishers, 1959.

Galilee was raised by Satan or his demons is considered sympathetically by such expositors as J. A. Alexander, R. C. Trench and J. N. Geldenhuys. Satan's use of natural forces within and without man's body, although strictly within the providence of God, is largely ignored by professing Christians today, and many find great difficulty in accepting it. But it was not always so. The older evangelical writers had no difficulty in accepting the fact that Satan does cause sorrow and suffering in the human race.

The Manipulation of Nations:

In view of Satan's power to afflict men's bodies and minds, to stir up antagonism among men (Job 1:14, 17), and to direct the forces of nature against men, although only as God permits him, we need not be surprised to find in Scripture an indication of his manipulation of nations and peoples. The present world system in its godlessness is often impelled by an evil supernaturalism. Thus in the tenth chapter of the prophecy of Daniel we read of 'the prince of the kingdom of Persia' who is the enemy of God and His people. As Edward J. Young writes, this 'prince' is not the king of Persia, 'for the thought here is that of spiritual warfare'.[10] In Daniel's vision, persecuting powers that sought the overthrow of Israel were influenced by a supernatural spiritual power, a spirit of evil. Indeed Daniel personally experienced the opposition of this 'prince' (v.13). He is the spirit-being who directs the desires and policies of the kingdom of Persia, and who, in particular, inflames this kingdom against Israel.

10. *Commentary on Daniel*, Banner of Truth Trust, 1972.

The Apostle Paul and his colleagues suffered much at the hand of pagan authorities. They were beaten and imprisoned. Yet behind the persecuting powers of earth, the Apostle clearly saw a more sinister enemy. 'We wrestle not', he wrote, 'against flesh and blood, but against principalities, against powers, against the rulers of the darkness of this world, against spiritual wickedness (wicked spirits) in high places' (Eph 6:12). Paul knew that it is against the Devil and all the demons under his command that we fight. We have to do with 'the wiles of the devil'. Alas! many Christians today are sadly naïve concerning those wiles. They forget that Satan is the arch-deceiver. He parades as an angel of light, or hides behind earthly governments and rulers, whichever suits his purpose best. He will even use a professed zeal for the study and understanding of the Bible to blind men to the very truth of that Word, as is clearly seen in the many cults professing to follow the teaching of Scripture. In Ephesians chapter 6 we see that Satan is not an obvious foe. Only the instructed believer can see his malice expressed in political terms and recognize his influence over earthly powers. Most men see only flesh and blood. As E. K. Simpson remarks, 'The father of lies works his deadliest havoc by "shamming dead" and writing his own obituary in unctuous terms; the wolf preys fellest when he masks himself in sheep's clothing.'[11]

Behind the dictators, the totalitarian systems, the persecuting powers, the capricious tyrants of this earth, the Bible sees Satan and his subalterns arrayed against mankind in general and the Church of God in particular. Who can say what spirit entered into the heart of an

11. Comments on Ephesians 6:12, *New London Commentary*, Marshall, Morgan & Scott, 1957.

Antiochus Epiphanes, a Nero or a Hitler? Admiral Donitz, war-time commander-in-chief of the German Navy, said of Hitler, thirty years later, 'He was a demon. He had a demonic character. The nature of a demon is that he succeeds in disguising the demonic side of himself and gives an impression of acting for the general good, so that you do not question his qualities. Like many of my generation I had great faith in Hitler and what he did to give Germany back its self-respect. I only fully realized the evil side of Hitler afterwards.'[12] The dependence of the Nazi leaders on the black arts is no secret. John Richards states that in 1940 'The British Secret Service enlisted the aid of the astrologer Louis de Wohl in an attempt to ascertain what astrological guidance Karl Krafft was giving the Fuehrer, for it was well known that Hitler based his decisions on this.'![13] There are times in history when civil violence and thirst for blood, not to mention those dark and dastardly deeds of cruelty which have stained the annals of our race, can only be adequately explained in terms of the demonic, the impelling, evil influence of the hosts of wickedness in the hearts of those that knew not God.

This sombre aspect of history is only seen in perspective when we view it against the background of the 'common grace' of a sovereign God. For in common grace, not only does the Spirit of God endow all men with talents and skills, He also restrains the evil that is in man, so that that evil never realizes its full potential in this life, and thus He curbs the violence of man's rebellion and keeps in bounds the tide of evil which otherwisew ould sweep

12. *The Daily Telegraph Magazine*, 33, October 26, 1973.
13. *But Deliver Us From Evil*, 27, Darton, Longman and Todd, 1974.

away the very fabric of society (Gen 20:6, 31:7, 2 Kings 19:27, 28, Rom 1:24, 26, 28, 13:1–4). The common grace of God subserves the purposes of His 'special grace' by which He redeems His people from their iniquities and gathers His elect from every nation and every age of time. It is clearly allied to the 'binding' of Satan and ensures on the basis of Christ's victory at Calvary that Satan and his minions can go so far and no farther in their depraved and destructive pursuits.

'The Power of Death':

In discussing the power and influence which Satan is permitted to exert in a sinful world, we must not overlook two passages – Hebrews 2:14, 15 and Ephesians 2:2 – which are often made to bear too great a weight. The former passage states that Christ partook of flesh and blood 'that through death he might destroy him that had the power of death, that is, the devil; and deliver them who through fear of death were all their lifetime subject to bondage.' On the basis of this text it has been asserted that Satan 'had the power of physical death'[14] and is to be regarded as 'executioner-in-chief'.[15] But while we freely admit that Satan can cause physical death if God permits him (Job 2:6), the power of death considered in Hebrews 2:14 is not Satan's ability to terminate life, but the tyranny which he exercises over the sinner through death. Consequently the writer goes on to speak of men being delivered from the bondage of

14. Merrill F. Unger, *Biblical Demonology*, 189, Scripture Press Publications, Inc., 1971.
15. See comment on Heb 2:14 by F. F. Bruce, note 80, *New London Commentary*.

this fear. The lives of the redeemed are not at the disposal of the devil, directly or indirectly. Our times are wholly in God's hand. Satan, however, was the introducer of sin and death among men, and, wherever he can, he terrorizes men with death, applying its *strength* and its *sting* mercilessly. Because of this fact, and because death is an integral part of the curse of God upon sin, death is termed 'the last enemy' (1 Cor 15:26) and it shall be destroyed with all the other 'works of the devil' (1 John 3:8).

'Prince of the Power of the Air':

The reference to Satan in Ephesians 2:2 as 'the prince of the power of the air' has been construed by some students to refer to a certain spatial domain of the Evil One and his forces. There was a time when some good people objected to aviation on the basis of this text! We have even seen the interpretation that the cloud which received the ascending Christ (Acts 1:9) was in fact a shield to protect His risen body as He passed through enemy territory! We would much prefer to interpret 'air' in Ephesians 2:2, with E. K. Simpson, as simply meaning 'the prevailing influence or surroundings amid which an individual or community breathes and moves'.[16] It corresponds to the 'spirit of the age' and agrees with the statement that 'the whole world lieth in the evil one' (1 Jn 5:19). There is no need to regard the passage in Ephesians as teaching that our planet is literally ensphered by satanic hosts. The Bible does not indicate any domain where Satan is sovereign.

16. *Commentary on Ephesians*, Marshall, Morgan & Scott, 1957.

Demons as Agents of Apostasy:

In the New Testament we find the demons already identified as agents of apostasy, seeking to corrupt the Christian Church either from within its visible borders or from without through cultic movements. Paul writes, 'Now the Spirit speaketh expressly, that in the latter times some shall depart from the faith, giving heed to seducing spirits, and doctrines of demons' (1 Tim 4:1-3). While it is true that some, including Calvin, understand 'seducing spirits' to mean teachers of false doctrine, the fact remains that such teachers are the dupes of evil spirits and their doctrines are the direct result of demonic influence. But it is by no means certain that the seducing spirits mentioned in this passage are teachers of falsehood. Expositors like Patrick Fairbairn and Hendriksen argue convincingly that the spirits in question are demons.[17] Apostasy is clearly associated with satanic intervention in 2 Thessalonians 2:9 where we read that the Man of Lawlessness comes with the power of Satan himself. As Leon Morris remarks, 'He is empowered by Satan to do Satan's work.'[18] The Apostle John in his first Epistle (4:1-6) sees false prophets as instruments of the Evil One. Through them the evil spirits find expression. John reminds his readers that there are many spiritual influences at work. He states that the test of spirits lies in their witness to the incarnation of Christ. He emphasizes the presence and threat of anti-Christianity with its false

17. *Commentary on the Pastoral Epistles*, Patrick Fairbairn, Zondervan Publishing House, 1956. *Exposition of the Pastoral Epistles*, William Hendriksen, Baker Book House, 1957.

18. *The Epistles of Paul to the Thessalonians*, Marshall, Morgan & Scott, 1959.

teaching about Christ, and assures believers that He who is in them is greater than he who is in the world. Once again the activity of the powers of darkness is associated with the teaching of false doctrine.

In Revelation 9:1–11 we are shown the interest of demons in the propagation of error in the minds of men in general. Here the demons are likened to locusts which damage, not the grass of the earth or the foliage of the trees, 'but only those men which have not the seal of God in their foreheads.' Their king is the 'angel of the abyss', Apollyon (destroyer). There is no reason to take the view of Merrill Unger that Apollyon is not Satan himself, but one of his princelings.[19] In this passage we have a picture of a satanic campaign to darken the minds of unregenerate men with error and so to corrupt their lives. Yet in this diabolical activity the demons are over-ruled by a sovereign God. Their destructive power is limited. They may 'torment' men for a season, but they may not 'kill' them. This spread of error is described in the opening verses of the chapter as a thick smoke which hangs like a pall darkening the light of the sun and filling the air that men breathe. It is a figurative way of describing the blotting out of the light of God's truth from men's minds and the darkening of their understanding, so that all their thinking rests upon presuppositions which are a flat contradiction of the revealed truth of God.

But more specifically, with reference to error within the professing Church, John links Satan and the demons with apostasy. Thus in Revelation 2:18–29 we have the burning words of Christ concerning 'that Jezebel of a woman', a false prophetess who seduced the members of

19. Ibid., p. 73.

the church at Thyatira to gross immorality and encouraged them to know 'the depths of Satan'. Archbishop Trench calls Jezebel 'the female Antichrist of the Old Testament',[20] and the seducer of the servants of Christ in Thyatira is branded with this name of infamy. She was the tool of the Evil One. From the letters to the churches at Smyrna and Philadelphia we learn that a church may so apostatize as to cease to be a true church of Christ, becoming instead a 'synagogue of Satan' (Rev 2:9, 3:9). James describes a bitter and haughty sectarianism which results from a wisdom which is not 'from above', but which is 'earthly, sensual, devilish' (lit. demoniacal) 3:15, and Weymouth translates: 'it belongs to the earth, to the unspiritual nature, and to evil spirits.' 'Its ultimate source', says Alexander Ross, 'is to be sought in the malignant demons of the pit.'[21] There is, then, a spurious wisdom which assails the Church, and which is declared to be not only not of God but demonic in origin. In the final analysis 'the spirit of truth and the spirit of error' (1 Jn 4:6) must be viewed as personal (cf. Jn 14:17). Indeed it is impossible to think of good and bad merely in abstract and non-personal terms. The moment we attempt to define or illustrate what is good or what is bad we enter the realm of the personal. That the spirit of error has an interest in apostasy and faction is clearly taught in Scripture, and we need to be able to affirm with the apostle Paul that 'we are not ignorant of his devices' (2 Cor 2:11).

20. *Commentary on Epistles to the Seven Churches in Asia*, 147. Kegan Paul, Trench, & Co., 1886.
21. *Commentary on the Epistles of James and John*, 69. Marshall, Morgan & Scott, 1954.

The Doom of Satan:

The final doom of Satan is vividly portrayed in the book of Revelation. Earnest Christians differ in their interpretation of parts of this book, but it is clear from chapter 20:7–10 that before our Lord returns, Satan will be allowed greater freedom of action. He will be 'loosed' and immediately he will launch a mighty onslaught against the Church of God. The Church is pictured in this passage as a 'camp' and a 'city'. She is seen as the object of Satan's last, wild attack. This assault will be comparatively short. It is described as a battle, not a war. Satan is to be 'loosed' for 'a little season' (Rev. 20:3). This is to be followed immediately by his final doom. Satan who had been so long 'bound' and cast into 'the abyss'[22] where he was shut up and sealed – all symbolical language indicating that by Christ's cross Satan had been despoiled, cast out and his influence firmly curtailed – having been permitted one final and desperate onslaught, will then be 'cast into the lake of fire and brimstone, where the beast and the false prophet are, and shall be tormented day and night for ever and ever' (Rev 20:10). This is the deepest hell, a place 'prepared for the devil and his angels' (Matt 25:41). It is most certainly not a place where Satan is in charge and torments others,

22. The word 'abyss', literally 'without bottom', is used in the New Testament to designate the abode of the dead, Hades, especially with reference to Satan and the demons; and it is depicted in the book of Revelation as a place of woe – Rom 10:7, Luke 8:31, Rev. 9:1, 2, 11; 11:7; 17:8; 20:1, 3. The relevant passages of Scripture indicate nothing more than that the demons are in a state of punishment and are under control. That their confinement is in no way inconsistent with a certain movement and activity is quite clear from Scripture as a whole.

an all-too-common idea. The doom of Satan is shared by the demons (Luke 8:31, Jude 6).

J. Marcellus Kik does not exaggerate when he writes: 'What a welcome will the Devil receive from those whom he has deceived! What curses, what vituperations, what abuses, what reviling, what berating will be heaped upon his head! He will be surrounded by a lake of curses. His nostrils cannot escape the stench of vituperation. It is part of his torment day and night. He will be hated, despised, and rejected throughout all eternity.'[23]

Satan's Present Wretchedness and Future Doom:

Total revolt against God and utter depravity can only mean an existence of indescribable wretchedness. It is impossible to read the Gospels carefully and not sense the abject misery and frustration of Satan and his demons. Their policy, as Patrick Fairbairn says, 'is characterized by mingled intelligence and blindness, cunning and folly, according as it is directed to those who, like themselves, are inclined to the evil, or to such as are wedded to the good: with the one it is skilfully laid and reaches its aim, with the other it perpetually miscalculates and defeats itself.' Fairbairn makes the point that as love and holiness are a moral necessity with the elect angels, sinning may be said to have become a moral necessity with these fallen beings. This is the outcome of utter depravity. Then he gives the following vivid and sobering quotation from the German theologian, Professor A. D. C. Twesten. 'Hence they are necessarily miserable. Torn loose from the universal centre of life,

23. *An Eschatology of Victory*, 248, The Presbyterian and Reformed Publishing Co, 1971.

without being able to find it in themselves; by the feeling of inward void, ever driven to the outward world, and yet in it irreconcilably hostile to it and themselves; eternally shunning, and never escaping, the presence of God; always endeavouring to destroy, and always compelled to promote His purposes; instead of joy in the beatific vision of the Divine glory, having a never-satisfied longing for an end they never reach; instead of hope, the unending oscillation between hope and despair; instead of love, an impotent hatred of God, their fellows and themselves: – can the fearful condemnation of the last judgment, the thrusting down into the bottomless pit of destruction (Rev 20:10), add anything to the anguish of such a condition, excepting that they shall see the kingdom of God for ever delivered from their assaults, their vain presumption that they can destroy or impede it scattered to the winds, leaving to them only the ever-gnawing despair of an inward rage, which cannot spend itself upon anything without, and is, therefore, for ever undeceived as to its own impotence!'[24]

The doom of Satan is a concomitant of the second coming of Christ. Then we shall see Satan's defeat at the Cross and his actual downfall *as one*. We shall see the lightning flash and hear the thunder simultaneously. We shall see the Cross in relation to time from God's standpoint; not at a point along a line with the past behind us and the future before us, but at the centre of a circle where the whole circumference may be viewed and where past and future are alike. At the end of time as we now know it,[25] we shall see it from an altogether new

24. *Hermeneutical Manual*, 228. T & T Clark, 1858.
25. For a discussion of time in the context of eschatology, see *The Return of Christ*, G. C. Berkouwer, pp. 39–46 etc.,

perspective, and while in eternity we shall remain finite creatures, we shall, nevertheless, view all history from the divine standpoint as we sing 'the song of Moses the servant of God, and the song of the Lamb, saying, Great and marvellous are thy works, Lord God Almighty; just and true are thy ways, thou King of saints' (Rev 15:3).

In view of Satan's crushing defeat at Calvary and his certain doom, it is unspeakably sad to see sinful men give him their allegiance and accept his lie. As W. J. Grier exclaims: 'How dreadful it is that multitudes are still slaves to this vanquished, convicted, sentenced being!'[26]

William B. Eerdmans Publishing Company, 1972, and on the finiteness of man in the next world and the consequent experience of some kind of duration, see *The Pauline Eschatology*, Geerhardus Vos, p. 290, Eerdmans, 1953.

26. *The Momentous Event*, 87, Belfast, 1945.

5

THE WITNESS OF THE OLD
TESTAMENT TO DEMONIC ACTIVITY

Although the phenomenon of demon-possession and the existence and activity of demons is not so prominent in the Old Testament as in the New, it is, nevertheless, a constant reality. The statement of some writers that demon-possession is almost unknown in the Old Testament, and was a phenomenon largely associated with the appearance of our Lord in history is not true to fact. The Old Testament contains clear references to Satan, demons, and their influence upon men.

Warnings Against Spiritism:

There are stern and frequent warnings against consorting with those who have 'familiar spirits' (Lev 19:31, 20:6; Deut 18:9–12; Isa 8:19, 19:3) and sorcerers and necromancers are condemned to death under Mosaic law. They practised divination with the assistance of evil spirits. The person referred to in the Old Testament as 'having a familiar spirit' corresponds to the 'medium' of modern spiritism, with her 'control'. The word translated 'witch' in the Bible really means a sorceress or medium. Because of the historical associations of the word 'witch' it is to be regarded as unsuitable for the purposes of our present study.

The Worship of Demons:

In addition to the references to those who had 'familiar spirits', the Old Testament also indicates the activity of demons in general, and the word for 'demon' is used in the Septuagint. The 'satyr' of Isaiah 13:21 and 34:14, a Hebrew word meaning 'a hairy creature', possibly a he-goat, is translated 'demon' in the Septuagint, and possibly these creatures were employed in some way for the manifestation of evil spirits or associated with demonism, a view supported by such commentators as Calvin, Luther, Barnes and Delitzsch, although J. A. Alexander favours the literal translation 'he-goat' and tends to regard the Septuagint as being in error at this point. The same word is translated 'devils' in the A.V. in Leviticus 17:7 ('sacrifices unto devils') and in 2 Chronicles 11:15 ('Jeroboam . . . ordained him priests for the high places, and for the devils'). The Septuagint also employs the word 'demon' in Isaiah 65:11 (A.V. 'troop'), where the meaning is obscure, and in Psalm 96:5 – 'All the gods of the heathen are demons' (A.V. idols). In this last passage the Hebrew indicates 'nothings' or nonentities. The same word is translated 'devils' in the A.V. in Deuteronomy 32:17 and Psalm 106:37 ('they sacrificed their sons and their daughters unto devils'). In both passages the Septuagint translates 'demons'. The Old Testament emphasizes the fact that the idols worshipped by the heathen have no true existence. In Isaiah 41:21 the idols are challenged to prove their deity. 'Let them bring forth and declare to us what is going to take place; as for the former events, declare what they were, that we may consider them, and know their outcome; or announce to us what is coming. Declare the things that are going to

come afterward, that we may know that you are gods . . .
Behold, you are of no account (lit., nothing), and your
work amounts to nothing. . .' The verdict at the end of
this chapter is clear, 'Their molten images are wind and
emptiness.' Again God says through Isaiah, 'Is there a
God beside me? yea, there is no God; I know not any.
They that make a graven image are all of them vanity;
and their delectable things shall not profit; and they are
their own witnesses; they see not, nor know; that they
may be ashamed' (chap. 44:8b–9).

The use of the word 'demon' by the Septuagint in
Psalm 96:5 is interesting in the light of 1 Corinthians
10:19–21. Paul reaffirms that an idol is nothing, but
teaches that the idolatry has been implanted in the minds
of men by demons, who take to themselves the worship
offered to idols. 'The things which the Gentiles sacrifice,
they sacrifice to demons, and not to God: and I would not
that ye should have communion with demons.' The
heathen did not intend to worship demons when they
sacrificed to idols, but in fact this is what they did (cf.,
Rev 9:20). Charles Hodge makes the point here that
'men of the world do not intend to serve Satan, when
they break the laws of God in the pursuit of their
objects of desire. Still in doing so they are really obeying
the will of the great adversary, yielding to his impulses,
and fulfilling his designs. He is therefore said to be the
god of this world.'[1] The gods of the heathen were
nonentities, imaginary beings (cf., 1 Cor 8:4–6), but the
sacrifices of the heathen were really offered to demons.
The translation of Psalm 95:6 and Psalm 106:37 in the
Septuagint, when viewed in the light of the passage in
1 Corinthians, is most significant. And who dare say that

1. Comment on 1 Corinthians 10:20.

the worship offered to modern idols is not in fact the worship of demons? Is not idolatry still the instrument of demons who seek to divert to themselves the worship owed to the Lord? Even in the cruder forms of idolatry which exist among primitive peoples, missionaries are constantly reporting a mysterious association between demonic manifestations and the actual material idol.[2]

Demons as Instruments of Punishments:

In Psalm 78:49 where we read of the plagues of Egypt, it is stated that God brought these troubles to pass by 'sending evil angels among them', and while grammatically this could mean 'angels who belong to the class of evil angels', as Hengstenberg points out,[3] it seems wiser to regard the angels in question as misfortune-bringing angels, in view of the fact that in Exodus 12, where we read of the destroying angel, there is no reference to evil angels and the 'destroyer' simply appears as the executor of God's judgment. It is true, however, that on other occasions in Old Testament history God did use demons to execute His plans for the punishment of the ungodly and disobedient. Wicked Ahab was punished by a 'lying spirit' which Jehovah put in the mouth of the prophets who led him to his ruin at Ramoth Gilead (1 Kings 22:23, cf., chap. 21:20, 25).

The case of Ahab as described in 1 Kings 22:20–22 and 2 Chronicles 18:21, 22, serves to illustrate further that the devil stands under God's power. Calvin comments,

2. See *Roaring Lion*, Robert Petersen, 29, 42, Overseas Missionary Fellowship, 1968.

3. Commentary on the Psalms, Vol II, 471, T & T Clark, 1864.

'When Ahab was to be deceived, Satan took upon himself to become a spirit of falsehood in the mouths of all the prophets, and commissioned by God, he carried out his task.' Calvin sees Satan as so ruled by God's bidding, 'as to be compelled to render Him service.' And he explains that he is not 'speaking of Satan's will, nor even of his effort, but only of his effect.' He sees Satan continually hostile to God, but 'because with the bridle of His power God holds him bound and restrained, he carries out only those things which have been divinely permitted to him; and so he obeys his Creator whether he will or not, because he is compelled to yield Him service wherever God impels him.'[4] We find a similar passage in Judges 9:23 where we read that 'God sent an evil spirit between Abimelech and the men of Shechem; and the men of Shechem dealt treacherously with Abimelech.' This must not be regarded merely as an evil disposition, but the influence of a demon. Similarly in the case of Saul, a literal translation of 1 Samuel 16:14–23 reads, 'The Spirit of the Lord turned aside from being with Saul and an evil spirit from the Lord fell upon (overwhelmed, assailed, terrified) him.' In the experience of Saul the expressions 'the Spirit of the Lord departed from Saul, and an evil spirit from the Lord troubled him' (1 Sam 16:14), 'came upon' him (18:10), and 'was upon' him (19:9) indicate a succession of *agencies* rather than dispositions. The effects resemble certain aspects of the behaviour of New Testament demoniacs.

The story of Saul (cf., 1 Sam 16:14; 13:8–14; 15:10–31) shows that he was responsible for the presence of his evil visitor. So was Ahab. But we would be wrong to conclude that all cases of demon-possession or attacks by demons

4. *Institutes*, Bk 1, 14, 17. S.C.M. Press, Ltd, 1961.

have been, or are, necessarily the result of immorality and abandonment to evil on the part of the victim. As we shall see when we come to consider the activity of demons in New Testament times, this is not so.

Heathen Influence:

In Psalm 106:37 we read that the Israelites on entering Canaan soon forgot their deliverance from Egypt and mingled with the heathen, learning their works, serving their idols and sacrificing their sons and daughters unto demons (cf., Deut 12:31; 32:17). This was the ultimate result of their idolatrous practices. In the light of 1 Corinthians 10, and bearing in mind the experience of missionaries in this respect, it is hard to believe that this gross form of idolatry was completely unattended by cases of demon-possession. This phenomenon has been consistently witnessed and reported by missionaries in China, Japan, India, Africa etc. From Leviticus 17:7 and Deuteronomy 32:17 we learn that some of the Israelites were involved in similar gross idolatry in Egypt, idolatry which made them the unwitting dupes of demons.

The Old Testament bears clear witness to demonic activity in the heathen nations, especially and significantly in ancient Egypt and Babylon. We have references to the magicians of Egypt performing wonders similar to some of those wrought by Moses, by means of 'enchantments' or secret arts. (Ex. 7:12, 22; 8:7, 18, 19). These passages do not record illustrations of current Jewish and Egyptian beliefs, but give a sober account of actual events that were inseparably linked with this critical period of Israel's history. The liberal view of the Biblical references to Satan and the demons is that it largely resulted, especially in the later stages of the Old Testament, from foreign influence, and that the New Testament inherited these beliefs and Christ accepted them as the framework in which He expressed His own mission. The fact is that the Biblical doctrine of Satan and his demons is radically different from the views of gods and spirits prevailing in pagan cultures, and even from the demonology current in Judaism in the days of our Lord.[5] Edersheim in his monumental *Life and Times of Jesus the Messiah*, refutes the notion that the angelology and demonology of the Bible are derived from even purely Jewish sources and asserts that the teaching of the New Testament on this subject 'represents, as compared with that of the Rabbis, not only a return to the purity of Old Testament teaching, but, we might almost say, a new revelation.'[6] Whatever the sources of current Jewish ideas of demonology in our Lord's time on earth, they in no way influence the teaching of Holy Scripture on the subject, and to suggest that the Scriptures simply reflect common Jewish beliefs which in turn were largely moulded by pagan cultures is to deny the whole concept of Divine revelation.

The Prevalence of Occultism:

Further references in the Old Testament to evil supernaturalism, are found in Daniel 1:20; 2:2, 27; 4:7, 9; 5:11, where we read of the influence of magicians and

5. The fact that Scripture presents but one archangel is proof that its doctrine of angels does not derive from Babylonian and Persian sources which taught that there were seven archangels.

6. Appendix XIII, Longmans, Green, & Co., 1887.

sorcerers in the Babylonian court. These people were employed to predict the future and unlock the secrets of the invisible world. In the pronouncement of God's judgments against Babylon and Chaldea there is express reference to these evils (Isa 47:9–13; cf., Ezek 21:21, 22). These ancient sorcerers, as in present times, made use of magic arts, of occult phemonena, and frequently this involved demon-possession. The 'witch' of Endor is described in the original as 'mistress of a demon' and generally, whether in Israel or in heathen lands, the sorcerer was in league with the sinister forces of darkness and had a familiar spirit which he served. This corresponds with the 'control' – 'medium' relationship of modern spiritism.[7]

The orgiastic rites of the priests of Baal (1 Kings 18:28) are strongly suggestive of demon-possession; and it is significant that Jezebel, that patroness of Baalism, was known to dabble in magical incantations (A.V. witchcraft, 2 Kings 9:22). God said through Micah, 'I will cut off witchcrafts out of thine hand, and thou shalt have no more soothsayers' (5:12). This suggests that the use of occult methods with all their attendant evils was by no means rare in Old Testament days, especially when idolatry was rife.

The references in the Old Testament to occultism are numerous. Manasseh encouraged demon-worship and occult practices in conjunction with idolatry (2 Kings 21:6, 7). There is a striking passage in Ezekiel 13:17–23 where certain would-be prophetesses are sternly denounced. Claiming the gift of prophecy (v.17) and pretending to be inspired by Jehovah (v.19), they were

7. The term 'control' in spiritist circles today is an abbreviation for 'control spirit'. Another term used is 'spirit guide'.

really sorceresses who, through the use of magic arts, and possibly immoral practices, sought to gain unlawful influence over those who consulted them. The passage is obscure. As H. L. Ellison remarks, 'It is impossible now to know with certainty what the rigmaroles of these women meant.'[8] Whether or not they practised magic by proxy, that is, by the use of small images or other articles representing their evil intent, so that from a distance they might exercise the desired influence, a method not unknown in those days, and still used by 'black witches' today, or whether the passage simply indicates their attempts to gain complete control over their dupes, the sinister and occult nature of their designs is quite evident.[9] There is no inherent power in the 'abracadabra' of magic, but it may become, and often does become, the gateway for evil spirits. Its downright superstition and implied atheism provide an atmosphere which is thoroughly congenial to the Evil One. It can become the conductor of the lightning of evil supernaturalism. It belongs to the apparatus of spiritism and as such is forbidden and condemned by God.

There are many references in the Old Testament to the wearing of charms, and the word translated 'earrings' really means a charm or enchantment (e.g., Isa 3:20). The word is associated with snake-charming, a practice not unknown in Old Testament times (Eccl 10:11). Possibly this charm was in the shape of a serpent.

8. *Men Spake from God*, 107, The Paternoster Press, 1966 edition. Compare Ellison's *Ezekiel the Man and his Message* (Paternoster, 1967 edition). The comments of G. A. Cook *in loco*, *International Critical Commentary*, are also helpful.

9. Compare the practices of similar women in Jerusalem, Jer 7:18; 44:17, 19.

Isaiah refers to women's ornaments and provides a list (3:18–23) including other charms: 'round tires like the moon', or moon-images (in Judges 8:21, 26 translated 'ornaments'); 'cauls', used only here in Scripture, but a similar word in the Ras Shamra tablets is thought to denote sun-pendants. There is a reference to charms in Genesis 35:2–4, where we read that Jacob's household put away their 'strange gods' and their 'ear-rings'. Here the normal word for ear-ring is used, but the association with idols suggests that they may have been charms. Throughout the centuries, charms have always been associated with idolatry, demon-worship and the resulting superstition.

The witness of the Old Testament to the reality of Satan and the demons is clear and unequivocal, and it shows the power and menace of demonism within Israel. The medium was a constant threat to true religion and to the souls who made use of her. With each and every decline in the spiritual life of Israel there came a corresponding increase of idolatry, demon-worship, demon-possession and associated occult practices. The Hebrews in Egypt had seen much of 'the depths of Satan' and had not always been unscathed by the withering power of demonic activity. The Hebrews were always aware of the practices and beliefs of their heathen neighbours and the Old Testament abounds with references to the idolatry and demon-worship of those nations. The Israelites knew why they were not to marry heathen women, such unions leading almost invariably to idolatry. Whatever differences in *theory* may have existed between disobedient Jews who dabbled in occultism, and their heathen neighbours, there was a great deal in common in their *practice* of the occult arts and the resulting spiritism. Repeatedly we read in the Old Testament that Israel 'went a whoring' after Baal and other heathen deities. 'They even sacrificed their sons and their daughters to the demons, and shed innocent blood, the blood of their sons and their daughters, whom they sacrificed to the idols of Canaan; and the land was polluted with the blood. And they became unclean in their practices, and played the harlot in their deeds.' (Psa 106:37–39).

God's Judgments on Spiritism:

The rise of spiritism in Israel was something which God would not tolerate. It called forth His stern yet merciful judgment, stern in its form and execution, yet merciful in its aim, namely the spiritual purification of His chosen people. The passage in Psalm 106 just quoted goes on to tell of God's holy anger against His people for their gross idolatry. 'Therefore the anger of the Lord was kindled against his people, and he abhorred his inheritance. Then he gave them into the hand of the nations; and those who hated them ruled over them' (vv. 40, 41). This whole psalm tells in detail of Israel's departure from the Lord and how they provoked Him with their deeds. All rebellion against God was a form of idolatry because of its self-will and proud spirit of self-sufficiency. Samuel said to the disobedient Saul, 'Rebellion is as the sin of witchcraft (soothsaying), and stubbornness is as iniquity (heathenism) and idolatry' (1 Sam 15:23). Man must serve a master. Either he will obey God or he will obey the Devil. God's chosen people will either prove a faithful wife or they will commit spiritual adultery, and this latter course God will not suffer. The practice of spiritism in ancient Israel was a capital offence. 'You shall not allow a sorceress to live' (Ex 22:18, cf., Lev. 20:6, 27). Everything that was spiritist or occult was forbidden by God: 'There shall not be found among you anyone who makes his son or his daughter pass through the fire, one who uses divination, one who practises witchcraft, or one who interprets omens, or a sorcerer, or one who casts a spell, or a medium, or a spiritist, or one who calls up the dead. For whoever does these things is detestable to the Lord; and because of these detestable things the Lord your God will drive them out before you' (Deut 18:10–12.).

It is clear that the exile of the Jews in Babylonia was due to persistent apostasy, and this apostasy reached its lowest depths in superstition and idolatry. Isaiah was used to expose this declension and in his prophecy there are specific references to spiritism (chp. 8:19, 20; 29:4). Jeremiah strikes the same note. To Zedekiah and his advisers he delivered a word of warning: 'Hearken not ye to your prophets, nor to your diviners, nor to your dreamers, nor to your enchanters, nor to your sorcerers, which speak with you saying, Ye shall not serve the king of Babylon' (27:9). But Zedekiah would not listen and refused to submit to the authority of Babylon and so came the final stage of the captivity. The Jewish leaders preferred the sorcerers' word to that of Jeremiah, and heavy judgment came upon them. If they had been guided by the word and Spirit of God all would have been well, but for generations the word of God had been eclipsed in their minds because it was unpopular and because the lies of their spiritist advisers (Jer 27:10) suited the inclinations of their hearts.

Abandonment to spiritism was, at times, a divine

judgment on a nation. Of Egypt God said, 'I will destroy the counsel thereof: and they shall seek to the idols, and to the charmers, and to them that have familiar spirits, and to the wizards' (Isa 19:3). But it was His gracious purpose to save His people from such darkness and shame and to give them a Prophet whose word would be their peace and salvation. The contrast between the nations that hearken unto the word of an evil supernaturalism and a covenant people who will hearken unto Christ is clearly drawn in Deuteronomy 18:14, 15. It is prefaced by the command, 'Thou shalt be perfect with the Lord thy God.'

Perhaps the greatest sign of God's judgments on idolatry and its underlying demonism, is the valley of Hinnom, called Gehenna in the New Testament. Situated outside Jerusalem, it was for long the main centre of Baal worship among the Jews. Here Manasseh had led the people in the most lascivious idolatry. He instituted a new priesthood, composed of sorcerers,[10] and proceeded to serve Molech, a form of idolatry with which the sacrifice of children in the fire had been long associated.[11] It is said that the victims were placed on the red-hot hands of the brazen idol, their shrieks being drowned by the clash of cymbals and the shouts of the worshippers. Milton wrote of that terrible place:

'First Moloch, horrid King, besmear'd with blood
Of human sacrifice, and parents' tears,
Though for the noise of drums and timbrels loud

10. See 2 Kings 21:6. The expression 'he made' implies, in the original, formal appointment.
11. For Biblical references to this practice see Lev 18:21, 20:2, 3, 4, 5; 2 Kings 23:10; Jer 32:35; cf., 2 Kings 17:31.

Their children's cries unheard, that past through fire
To his grim idol. . . .'[12]

When the good King Josiah began his sweeping reforms,
this dreadful place was ceremonially defiled in order that
the cult of Molech might never be re-established there
(2 Kings 23:10). Where formerly those fires of cruel
idolatry burned, now fires of another kind were to burn.
The Valley of the Sons of Hinnom was to become the
refuse dump of Jerusalem. Here dead carcasses of beasts
and all offal were to be cast, and left to be devoured by
that worm that never dieth and that fire that is never
quenched. And so it came to be used as the name of the
place where the wicked are to be punished in the world
to come – Gehenna, translated 'hell' in our Bible. It is in
hell that Satan, the demons and all their devotees are
punished for ever. 'Gehenna . . . where their worm
dieth not, and the fire is not quenched' (Mark 9:43, 44).

12. *Paradise Lost*, Bk I. The valley of Hinnom was also
called Tophet, variously understood as meaning a drum, a place
of burning or a place of spitting (i.e., an object of abhorrence).

6

THE WITNESS OF THE NEW
TESTAMENT TO DEMON-POSSESSION

When we commence to read the New Testament we are immediately confronted by demon-possession as a well-known affliction. Frequently we read of Christ casting out demons, and symptoms or physical manifestations of possession are clearly indicated. The New Testament throughout is profoundly aware of the activity of the demons and of the forces of darkness marshalled against the Son of God and His Church on earth. Conflict with evil powers is mentioned some fifty times in the Gospels alone. As to the alleged silence of the Gospel of John on this subject, we observe that while that Gospel does not report any healing of a demon-possessed person, it shares the same over-all view of Satanic power as the other Gospels (Jn 7:20; 8:48–52; 10:20, 21).

Demon worship was an established phenomenon in the Greek and Roman world in New Testament times. Festus pronounced the charges of the Jews against Paul to be 'a question of their own demon worship' (Acts 25:19, Gk. The word is usually translated 'superstition'). Paul considered the Athenians noteworthy for their worship of demons (Acts 17:22, Gk.).

The Reality of Demon-Possession:

The diminutive word for demon, daimonion, is used by Matthew eleven times, by Mark thirteen times, by Luke twenty-two times in his Gospel and once in Acts. Twice Matthew uses the term 'unclean' as descriptive of 'spirit';

Mark does so eleven times and Luke five times in his Gospel, applying the term 'unclean' to demon once. Twice Luke applies the adjective 'evil' to spirit; and in Acts he uses 'unclean' twice and 'evil' four times with reference to spirit. The word daimon (demon) occurs less frequently in the Gospels, and the verb 'to be demonized' occurs seven times in Matthew, four times in Mark, once in Luke and once in John. Quite clearly the Gospels are at one in their presentation and exposure of demonic activity. As we would expect to find in the inspired record of a divine revelation, there is complete harmony on this as on all other subjects discussed.

The physical manifestations of possession indicated in the New Testament include hypochondria, insanity, epilepsy (a word coming from the Greek for 'seizure', lit. 'to seize'!), frenzy, impediment of speech, dumbness, deafness and blindness. The demoniac is seen to have one or more of these afflictions, and there is something more than the usual symptoms of an ailment. He speaks in a way that is unusual for ordinary sufferers (Matt 8:29, Mark 1:24) and often possesses supernatural strength, Mark 5:4, Acts 19:16. No mental illness is indicated in the case of the dumb man in Matthew 9:32 or in the case of the blind and dumb man in Matthew 12:22, yet both men were demon-possessed. In Matthew 17:15–18, Mark 9:17 and Luke 9:39, epileptic symptoms are attributed to demonic activity.[1]

The writers of the New Testament, like the Jewish people of their day, distinguish between ordinary cases of illness and illness which was merely symptomatic of something much more sinister. They distinguished

1. 'The Case of the Epileptic Boy', *The Expository Times*, Vol. LXXIX. No. 2.

between ordinary illness and demon-possession (Mark 1:32, 34; Matt 8:16).[2] They even distinguished between ordinary madness and possession (Matt 4:24). We read of numerous cases of people who suffered from such afflictions as deafness, dumbness and blindness, who were in no way possessed of demons (e.g., Mark 7:32). This is important in view of the liberal interpretation of New Testament references to possession as the manner of explaining diseases such as insanity, epilepsy and melancholia, which were prevalent at that time. This theory simply does not fit the facts as we find them in the Gospels. The Jews were well aware of the strange and terrifying differences between certain cases of illness and others which often had the same symptoms but lacked the sinister aspect known only in the demoniac.

In the New Testament the demoniacs freely confess that they are possessed (Mark 5:9) and their near-of-kin agree (Matt 15:22). On the other hand it must be borne in mind that it is the demon who speaks in such cases, not the possessed, although the latter becomes the instrument of the demon's response.[3] There is abundant evidence from missionaries to show that, after attacks of demon-possession, the victim has no memory whatever of what he said or did. He may, for example, have spoken in a language he had never heard, and yet later will have no memory of having done so. Missionary accounts show that this particular phenomenon is by no means rare; and neither, for that matter, is the healing of the sick by means of demonic agencies. Healings at spiritist meetings and Christian Science gatherings are also regular occurrences.

2. A. Rendle Short, *The Bible and Modern Medicine*, 117, Paternoster Press, 1955.
3. Ibid., 111.

The Nature of Demon-Possession:

In the New Testament demon-possession is a stark, stern reality, the tormented, raving demoniacs being introduced frequently. It is necessary for us to examine the examples of possession which are given in the New Testament, to note the salient features in each case, and to seek to learn what is peculiar to each case.

(a) *The demoniacs in the country of the Gadarenes:*
(Matt 8:28–34, Mark 5:1–20, Luke 8:26–39).

We are not concerned in this study with the difficulty that Matthew speaks of two demoniacs, while Mark and Luke speak only of one, or that Matthew lays the scene of the miracle in the country of the Gergesenes, while Mark and Luke place it in that of the Gadarenes. Suffice it to say here that there were two demoniacs and that one comes to the fore; he may well have been the fiercer of the two. Yet they were both in the same plight, and in dealing with one of them, after the style of Mark and Luke, we in fact discuss the experience of both. The picture of this wretched man is indeed fearful to behold. Each of the Evangelists recording this case adds his own touch. Mark's account is exceptionally vivid. We see the possessed wandering naked among the tombs, where he found shelter and at the same time scope for his deranged imagination. Besides, the Jews believed that evil spirits dwelt especially in deserts and among tombs, and a possessed Jew would still behave in a general way according to his Jewish beliefs and superstitions. At the sight of the Lord, and upon His command to the unclean spirit to depart, the man cried out and fell before Him, saying in a loud voice, 'What have I to do with thee, Jesus, thou Son of the Most High God? I beseech thee, torment me not.' This was the demon speaking through the possessed, or, more accurately, the demons, for the man who called himself 'Legion', was possessed by many demons. The salient features of this sad case are a life of misery and violence, frequent seizures and displays of phenomenal strength, immediate recognition of the Saviour on the part of the indwelling spirits coupled with fear and the confession of their certain doom, and the inability of the demons to defy the command of Christ. They have no choice but to obey Him. So far as the victim is concerned, we see his whole personality mastered by the invading spirits, resulting in a strange confusion, so that he wandered as a raving maniac, a danger to himself and to others. His own individuality was suppressed and he was virtually the instrument of his torturers. Even so there was a flicker of self-awareness. When asked his name he was able to reply. Most commentators are of the opinion that the question was addressed to the man in order to assist him to realize that he was a distinct personality, although his answer showed how confused he was in this respect. It was as if he had said, 'I am many'. Indeed the very answer is one of conflict, '*My* name is Legion, for *we* are many' (Mark 5:9). A Roman legion usually consisted of six thousand men, and the name Legion in this account indicates the invasion of this man's personality by many demons (cf., Luke 8:2). In seeking permission to enter the swine the evil spirits thought to escape their prison-house, the 'abyss', but not so. The swine perished and the demons were still imprisoned, still within the abyss. As Godet reminds us, 'Their request to

4. See Rendle Short, Ibid., 111ff.

enter into the swine only refers . . . to the way by which
they were suffered to go into the abyss.'[5] Christ made no
response to their request not to send them there, and one
reason for the way they were permitted to leave may
well have been to demonstrate to all concerned, especially
the man himself, that this particularly vicious possession
was at an end, the demons having really gone. Of one
thing we may be quite certain, the permission for the
demons to enter the swine was not granted for the
benefit of the demons. Finally, we see the man completely
restored. He is freed from evil spirits; he sits calmly at the
feet of his Deliverer; he is clothed; he is in full possession
of his senses and he is completely sociable again. Now he
must return to his people and tell what great things God
had done for him.

There has been a measure of speculation in the
exposition of the passages which record this miracle. It is
frequently suggested that demons yearn for some kind of
physical contact and that part of their misery consists in
being deprived of a material form, hence their desire to
embody themselves in some way or other. It is much
more probable that their interest in material contacts is
purely destructive and part of their general hostility to
God and His creation. It is also suggested that their
request to be allowed to enter the swine was malicious
and had the object of turning the people against Christ.[6]
This may or may not have been the case. The view that
Christ permitted the demons to enter and destroy the

5. *Commentary on Luke*, Vol I. 386. Zondervan Publishing
House.

6. This view is expressed by J. A. Alexander, who sees the
request of the demons as a sample of their 'craft and cunning'.
Commentary on Mark, Banner of Truth Trust, 1960.

swine partly as an expression of His indignation at the sight of a herd of animals which the Jews were forbidden to keep, overlooks the fact that this particular district was as much Gentile as Jewish, and the owners of the swine may well have been Gentiles. It seems wiser to view the matter in the light of Christ's words, 'How much is a man better than a sheep?' For some reason not known to us it was necessary in this case to destroy these animals for the sake of the sufferer.

(b) *The demoniac in the synagogue of Capernaum:* (Mark 1:23–27; Luke 4:31–36).

In this instance Christ taught in the synagogue on the Sabbath and His hearers were profoundly impressed by the commanding character of His teaching. It was unique and utterly different from what the people were accustomed to hear. He spoke definitely and with authority, not the authority of old-time sages and commentators, but with His own authority. As W. F. Arndt remarks, 'He did not preach "open questions" but "demanded acceptance of what He proclaimed".'[7] In the context of this preaching, a demonic presence was suddenly in evidence. A man in the congregation who was possessed of an unclean demon, cried out, 'Let us alone; what have we to do with thee, thou Jesus of Nazareth? art thou come to destroy us? I know thee who thou art; the Holy One of God.' The man had become the mouthpiece of the demon. A literal translation of this remarkable utterance would read, 'Ah! What is there between us and thee, Jesus Nazarene? Camest thou to destroy us? I know thee who thou art, the Holy One of God.' Godet observes that

7. *Commentary on Luke*, 142, Concordia Publishing House, 1956.

the cry 'Ah!' is equivalent to 'let be!' and likens it to 'that of a criminal who, when suddenly apprehended by the police, calls out: Loose me!'[8], or in present-day speech, 'Let me go.' The response of the Saviour to this outburst was equally emphatic. 'Jesus rebuked him, saying, Hold thy peace, and come out of him.' It was a terse, stern reply. What He said was, 'Be muzzled and come out from him.' It is the expression which our Lord used when He rebuked the storm on Galilee (Mark 4:39) and was a command of power. There was a terrible convulsion as the demon withdrew, but there was no permanent injury of the man. Great was the astonishment of the onlookers. 'What a word is this!' they said. 'What *teaching* is this!' For in the light of Luke 4:32 we are obliged to take the term 'word' here as meaning the preaching of Christ in general. It was not the actual command to the demon that was the object of their astonishment, although that in itself was wonderful, but the authoritative preaching accompanied by power so great that the demonic presence in that assembly was driven to reveal itself and then peremptorily expelled. The authority by which Christ taught was backed by a power (v.36 dunamis) which compelled the very demons to render obedience. Christ was master in deed as well as in name. Mark makes the people say, 'What new doctrine is this?' It was as if they had exclaimed, 'Here is something new!'

(c) *The demon-possessed Syrophenician girl:* (Matt 15:21–28; Mark 7:24–30).

A Gentile woman came to Christ beseeching Him to cast the demon out of her 'young daughter' who had an

8. Ibid., 245.

unclean spirit which caused the girl terrible distress. Matthew's account informs us that the girl was 'grievously vexed with a demon', or as it may be literally rendered, she was 'badly demonised'. The immediate response of the Lord appeared to be unsympathetic, even harsh. 'Let the children first be filled; for it is not meet to take the children's bread, and to cast it unto the dogs.' It is not our present purpose to reflect upon the wonderful conversation between Christ and this woman and the astounding faith which she evinced. It is the granting of her request which now concerns us; although there is undoubtedly an important link between this faith, brought about by the word and Spirit of Christ, and the ensuing miracle. The command of Christ was as potent when expressed at a distance, as when He was physically present. His will was immediately obeyed by the unclean spirit. The mother returned to find her daughter weak but calm as she lay on the bed where the departing spirit had *thrown* her (A.V. 'laid'). The miracle of dispossession had been sudden and complete. Her tormentor had gone, cast out by the irresistible authority of the Son of God.

(d) *The demoniac boy:* (Matt 17:14–21, Mark 9:14–29, Luke 9:37–42)

The physical symptoms of this distressing case of demon-possession are described by Mark and Luke. They include severe convulsions, foaming at the mouth, grinding of the teeth, dumbness, deafness, rigidity of the body and wasting away or exhaustion. The attacks came on suddenly, and frequently the demon would cast the boy into fire and into water to destroy him. Those apostles who had not accompanied Christ to the scene of the Transfiguration tried to expel the demon but failed.

They had been given power to expel demons but this was an exceptional case and it would appear from Mark 9:29 that their faith may have faltered when confronted by so powerful and violent a demon as this. The intense malignity of this evil spirit is seen in his violent reaction as the lad is brought to the Saviour. 'When he was still approaching, the demon threw him down and convulsed him' (Luke 9:42). As Christ rebuked the 'foul spirit', saying 'Thou dumb and deaf spirit, I charge thee, come out of him, and enter no more into him', the demon withdrew as violently as possible. Mark tells us that he 'cried, and rent him sore, and came out of him, and he was as one dead; insomuch that many said, He is dead' (9:26). Luke concludes his account with the words, 'And all were amazed at the majesty of God.' Just as a retreating army will burn and destroy as much as possible before evacuating its position, so this enemy exerted the utmost malice of which he was capable as he reluctantly obeyed the Christ of God.

The symptoms are clearly those of epilepsy, but plainly in this instance they were produced by a deeper and more sinister malady. Whether or not the expression 'this kind' (Mark 9:29) indicates a demon more powerful than others, such a distinction is implied in the term 'principalities and powers' (Eph 6:12, cf., Luke 11:26). Missionaries report that the degree of a witch doctor's effectiveness as a sorcerer depends on the authority of his familiar spirit. In heathen communities sorcerers are often graded according to their efficacy as mediums, the rank of demons being reflected in the ranks of the sorcerers.[9] It should be noted, in passing, that not everyone who is possessed with an evil spirit has a familiar spirit.

9. Robert Petersen, ibid., 106ff.

It is only when a person willingly seeks to become an agent of the demon, as in spiritism and magic, that the spirit may be termed 'familiar'. In such cases there is full co-operation between the demon and the agent. We must, therefore, distinguish between voluntary possession and involuntary possession. In the latter case there has been no desire for demonic possession, and possibly no awareness of it. The 'demoniac boy', like the Syrophenician girl, is an example of involuntary possession. A significant feature of Mark's account of this miracle is his inclusion of Christ's word to the departing spirit, 'enter no more into him'. Exorcism was practised by the Jews (Luke 11:19), and is still practised by sorcerers, but the demon can return at will and usually does so. Christ did not practise exorcism in the modern sense of the word. He bade the demons depart and never return, commands they had no choice but to obey.

(e) *The Dumb Demoniac:* (Matt 9:32–34). *The Blind and Dumb Demoniac:* (Matt 12:22–30).

The story of the healing of the dumb demoniac is peculiar to Matthew's Gospel. Elsewhere we read of cures of the deaf and dumb and the blind, where no demon-possession was involved (Mark 7:31–37; John 9; Matt 9:27, 20:30). But then there are examples of these afflictions resulting from possession. The terms 'dumb spirit', and 'deaf spirit', in the Gospels, indicate a spirit causing dumbness or deafness. In Matthew 9:32 we have the case of a man who was rendered dumb by a demon and when Christ cast out the demon the man spoke. In Matthew 12:22 we read of a possessed man who was both blind and dumb. When he was delivered from the evil power he could speak and see. The value of these miracles in our present study is that they show very clearly that demon-possession was not an ordinary physical disease. There was no functional disorder in either of these cases, and the onlookers were well aware of this. The deafness, dumbness and blindness were only the physical manifestations of a demonic presence which had invaded and afflicted the human body as well as the mind.

(f) *The slave-girl at Philippi:* (Acts 16:16–18).

The slave-girl at Philippi is said to have been possessed with a 'spirit of divination' (Python), and the language indicates more than an unbalanced mind. This demon-possessed girl was regarded as a 'pythoness', a person inspired by the god Apollo who was worshipped as the 'Pythian' god at the shrine of Delphi or Pytho in central Greece. As her involuntary utterances were regarded as the voice of this god she was in constant demand and brought much gain to her masters. F. F. Bruce points out that Plutarch, the Greek philosopher and biographer (A.D. 46–120), calls these people 'ventriloquists, whose utterances were really and not apparently beyond their conscious control.'[10] The same Greek word is used in the Septuagint of those who had 'familiar spirits', for example, the witch of Endor. The word 'ventriloquist' means 'speaking from the belly' (*venter*, the belly; *loqui*, to speak), and this is precisely what happens in certain forms of demon-possession. But not in all! It will not suffice, therefore, to dismiss those in the Old Testament who had 'familiar spirits' as mere ventriloquists in the modern sense of the term. The significant aspect of this case is that the testimony of the demon to the mission of

10. Acts, *New London Commentary*, Marshall, Morgan & Scott, Ltd., 1954.

Paul and his companions seemed to be on the side of God and His truth; but in fact it was not, and Paul, recognizing the real source of this pseudo-prophecy, firmly challenged the spirit and bade him in the name of Jesus Christ to depart from the girl, a command that was immediately obeyed. That the forces of darkness frequently pose as angels of light (2 Cor 11:14) is never to be forgotten by the servants of the Lord.

These are the main examples of demon-possession recorded in the Gospels and in Acts. By examining them carefully against the background of the whole of Scripture, we are enabled to form a general impression of the nature of demon-possession in New Testament times:

(1) Demon-possession may be voluntary or involuntary.

(2) There is no *essential* link between the character of the victim and his possession.

(3) Possession may be permanent or spasmodic, the former case being illustrated by Luke 11:26 where the word translated 'dwell' indicates permanent residence.

(4) Body and mind alike are affected. There is either a general suppression of the personality, or the emergence of a kind of double personality. In either case, the victim becomes the instrument of the demon. Consequently it is the demon who speaks through the instrumentality of the person possessed.

(5) Symptoms vary greatly, but frequently include, especially in cases of involuntary possession, mental abnormality, epileptic or similar fits, superhuman strength, suicidal tendencies and a malignant attitude towards others. Sometimes there is an uncanny recognition of the presence of Christ and an acute awareness of His Person and authority.

(6) Deliverance, when it comes, is sudden.

Missionaries have prepared lists of symptoms found in possessed persons and they correspond with those found in the Bible.[11] In addition they report speech in a language unknown to the victim, genuine cases of healing, rappings, apparitions, the moving of solid objects through space, said to result from the activity of 'poltergeists' or 'noisy spirits')[12] and so forth, such physical phenomena being frequently associated with demonism and Satan worship as found today in spiritist circles all over the world.

It has been urged that in cases of possession the demon comes between the soul and the body as a foreign influence. Consequently the bodily organs of the soul suffer and the soul loses control of them. On this view the demon does not take up his habitation in the soul, nor directly influence the spiritual nature, but attacks the nervous system and works through it, producing the familiar symptoms of possession. J. H. A. Ebrard, who defends this view, states that 'demoniacal agency is not exerted through the spiritual upon the moral . . . but through the physical upon the rational nature'.[13] It is also stated that possession may be either physical or spiritual.[14] But it is impossible to tear apart body and

11. See Nevius, ibid., 143 and Petersen, Ibid., 116.

12. In connection with the Wesleys, it is interesting to note that the Epworth parsonage was supposed to have a poltergeist and John Wesley wrote an account of it. The children called it 'Old Jeffrey'. There have been numerous cases of furniture moving, stones flung through the air, crockery smashed, etc.

13. *Schaff-Herzog Encyclopaedia of Religious Knowledge*, Vol 1, 624, Funk & Wagnalls Company, 1891.

14. This is the view of A. H. Strong, *Systematic Theology*, 456, The Judson Press, 1907.

soul in this particular context. In a human being there is an interaction of body and soul, of the material and the spiritual. The demoniacs of the New Testament were affected both materially and spiritually and it is unwise to be dogmatic where detailed information is lacking.

Possession, and in special, involuntary possession, must be distinguished from yielding to temptation. In yielding to temptation the will submits itself consciously, and by yielding gradually assumes, without losing its freedom of action, the characteristics of the satanic nature. It is influenced and persuaded, but never overborne. Demon-possession is totally different. The attack can be sudden and irresistible. It results in the complete or partial loss of the sufferer's reason or power of will. His thoughts and actions are controlled by the evil spirit until his personality is completely submerged and overborne, producing either a two-fold consciousness (e.g., 'My name is Legion: for we are many' Mark 5:9), or a total loss of self-awareness. It is common in our time to find that after an attack the victim has no memory of what he said or did while possessed. In other cases the victim will speak at one moment as the person he is, and in the next moment the demon will speak through the victim. In both aspects the sufferer is at the mercy of a ruthless power. The demon functions through the mind and body of the possessed person (Luke 4:33–34), which he has usurped, so that self-destruction sets in; there is a perversion of humanity and the man or woman becomes a mere travesty of what it means to be a man or woman.

It is interesting to observe that we never read in Scripture of a person being possessed by the Devil, always by a demon or demons. We do, however, read that Satan 'entered into Judas', which at least must mean that Satan impelled him to act as he did (cf., Jn 13:2). There is nothing in Judas' conduct to suggest that he became a demoniac and was unable to control his actions. He appears as a willing accomplice of the Evil One in that he does what his heart wants to do, and in the first instance it was Judas who opened the door to Satan. Geldenhuys comments that Judas' treachery was the result of his 'inward estrangement from the Lord', and so he became 'completely under the sway of the Evil One and was thus incited to commit such black treachery'. And he quotes Zahn as saying that the word translated Satan (Luke 22:3) is without the article and is not to be taken as a proper name but as a generic name.[15] On one occasion Christ called Judas 'a devil' (Jn 6:70) for he was the tool of Satan.[16]

It is often stated that demon-possession only happens where there has been a life of almost total moral abandonment and that there is a definite connection between the character of the possessed and his unhappy condition. It is probably true to say that in very many instances such a connection between character and possession exists, but the case of the possessed Syrophenician girl and that of the demoniac boy make it abundantly clear that there is no essential connection between the two. Certain men and women have been excessively wicked and yet have shown none of the characteristics of the demoniac. On the other hand cases are known where mild and inoffensive people have suffered greatly as the result of demon-possession, as many missionaries can testify. The distinction between wicked men and demoniacs was clearly recognized in the early Church; there were excommuni-

15. Ibid., 548ff.
16. See Appendix (A).

cations for the former and exorcists for the latter. 'We must', says Trench, 'esteem the demoniac one of the unhappiest but not, of necessity, one of the guiltiest of our race.'[17]

The oft expressed view that spirits cannot possess a person without invitation is clearly contradicted by the Biblical evidence. This is not to deny that any form of invitation is exceedingly dangerous. In the final analysis, demon-possession results from the fall of man and the sinful condition of the race; it originates in a realm of evil which mankind is quite powerless to resist. We cannot agree with A. H. Strong's assessment of the Biblical data relating to demon-possession which leads him to conclude that 'the power of evil spirits over men is not independent of the human will. This power cannot be exercised without at least the original consent of the human will, and may be resisted and shaken off through prayer and faith in God.'[18] We may contrast with that statement the view of Pastor Hsi, who had considerable experience of demon-possession and whose own wife was once possessed. Hsi believed that all unregenerate men were more or less under the power of the devil. The spirit that now worketh in the children of disobedience has not in all cases manifested his full malice and cruelty, but of his actual dominion in the lives of those who do not belong to Christ, Hsi had no doubt (cf., Acts 26:18, 2 Tim 2:26, Eph 2:2)[19] Strong's reference to demonic power being 'shaken off through prayer and faith in God' would presuppose a state of regeneration and this leads us to the

17. *The Miracles of Our Lord*, 169, Macmillan & Co, 1874.
18. Ibid., 457ff.
19. *Pastor Hsi*, Mrs Howard Taylor, 160, Overseas Missionary Fellowship (reprint of 1967).

vital question as to whether a Christian can be demon-possessed.

Can a Christian be Demon-possessed?

In the light of Scripture we are compelled to reject the view that the Holy Spirit and an evil spirit can co-exist in the same person. Attempts to prove the contrary on the basis of observations are valueless. Human judgment is always fallible and must never be given priority over the teaching of the Word of God. When missionaries provide 'examples' of 'believers' being possessed, two questions immediately arise: Were the victims regenerate? Were they actually possessed? Passages of Scripture sometimes used to support this view prove no such thing. There is no reason to believe that the person 'delivered unto Satan for the destruction of the flesh, that the spirit may be saved' (1 Cor 5:5) was demon-possessed. This is also true of 1 Timothy 1:20 which refers to those 'delivered unto Satan, that they may learn not to blaspheme'. Those discussed in 2 Timothy 2:26 and said to be 'taken captive' by the devil 'at his will', are not believers at all.

The Biblical doctrines of regeneration and the permanent indwelling of the believer by the Holy Spirit make demon-possession of a believer utterly impossible. We are not asking if a *professing* Christian can be demon-possessed, but if a regenerate person can be possessed. The answer to this question is firmly in the negative. The man in Christ is 'born again' (Jn 3:5); He is a 'new creation' in Christ (2 Cor 5:17). He is part of the body of Christ (Eph 1:23). He is sealed by the Holy Spirit unto the day of redemption (Eph 4:30). He is permanently indwelt by the Holy Spirit (Rom 8:9). He is the temple of the Holy Spirit (1 Cor 6:19). The evil principalities and powers cannot separate him from the love of God which is in Christ Jesus (Rom 8:38, 39). The One who is in him is greater than the one who is in the world (1 Jn 4:4). Such a person cannot be indwelt by a demon. The Holy Spirit and an evil spirit cannot be joint occupants of the same heart. 'What concord hath Christ with Belial? . . . And what agreement hath the temple of God with idols? for ye are the temple of the living God . . .' (2 Cor 6:15, 16). The term *naos*, translated 'temple' in this passage, was used of the innermost sanctuary of the temple where the Divine presence was manifested. Paul places Christ and Satan, idols and the temple of God, in juxtaposition, as deadly antagonists. The antithesis is radical and absolute, as great as that between light and darkness (v.14). Believers are 'in Christ', and Christ is 'in' them (2 Cor 5:17, Eph 3:17, Col 1:27). It is altogether impossible for those who are 'Christ's' (1 Cor 3:23) to be Satan's. 'We are the Lord's', and we can belong to none other. The Christian cannot be demon-possessed. Such a notion contradicts everything which the New Testament has to say concerning the nature of the new birth and the standing of the child of God. 'It is impossible', says Martin Luther, 'for Jesus Christ and the devil ever to remain under the same roof. The one must yield to the other – the devil to Christ.'[20]

20. *Table Talk*, Hazlitt's translation, 83, David Bogue, 1868.

7

CHRIST AND THE DEMONS

The Authority of Christ over the Demons:

In the examples of demon-possession recorded in the New Testament, we have abundant evidence of the absolute authority of Christ over Satan and his underlings. He provided certain information about the demons (Matt 12:25, 26; 17:21), and regarded deliverance from possession as part of His ministry and a sign of His kingdom. 'If I with the finger of God cast out demons, no doubt the kingdom of God is come upon you.' In other words, where Satan's tyranny is destroyed, there of necessity the kingdom of God begins. Later, Peter was to proclaim the fact that Jesus of Nazareth 'went about doing good, and healing all that were oppressed of the devil' (Acts 10:38). In doing this our Lord always distinguished between the man and the demon. To the one He was compassionate and kind, to the other, stern and relentless. This distinction is obvious in His words to the Gadarene demoniac: 'Come out of the man, thou unclean spirit' (Mark 5:8). In keeping with this distinction, the victims of possession are said to be 'healed', while the demons are said to be 'cast out'. (Matt 8:16, Luke 6:18). We note the dread hostility of the demons in the presence of Christ. They confess His power, recognize His Deity and show an awareness of their doom. 'I know thee who thou art, the Holy One of God' is the confession of the demons. 'Art thou come to destroy us?' (Mark 1:24, Luke 4:34). 'Art thou come hither to torment us before the time?' (Matt

8:29). Demons are never agnostics. 'The demons also believe and shudder', wrote James in his Epistle (2:19). Alexander Ross comments, 'Their belief in the existence of God begets in them only a shivering fear and a horrible dread; it does not lead them to trust in God and it does not inspire in them loving service to Him.'[1] We see an expression of the same knowledge in the case of the slave-girl at Philippi. Through her the demon described Paul and his companions as 'servants of the most high God, which shew unto us the way of salvation' (Acts 16:17).

The truth is that while the hosts of darkness constantly seek to engender unbelief in the mind of man, they themselves have a certain knowledge of God which precludes all agnosticism on their part. Indeed it would appear that in the presence of Christ the evil spirits cannot remain silent, but must confess His Person and power and their own doom. As Edersheim says, 'The Christ needs not to contend: that He is the Christ, is itself victory.'[2] 'Nothing', writes J. L. Nevius, 'has excited more surprise in connection with these manifestations in China, than the fact that the subjects of these manifestations have in some cases evinced a knowledge of God, and especially of our Saviour; and acknowledged our Saviour's authority and power. The correspondence of this fact with the statements of Scripture is apparent.'[3] This same awareness of the Person and authority of Christ expressed through the instrumentality of the possessed has been repeatedly observed and recorded by missionaries since Nevius' day.

It is not surprising, then, to find that demoniacs rarely

1. Epistles of James and John, 52, *New London Commentary*, Marshall, Morgan & Scott, 1954.
2. Ibid., Vol. 1, 484.
3. Ibid., 257.

came to Christ of their own accord; they were, with one exception, brought to Him by their relatives and friends. Even in that exceptional case, the antipathy and terror of the demons were extreme (Mark 1:23–26). We are conscious of a fiendish rage balanced only by terror when the demoniac is in the presence of the Son of God.

There is a definite contest between the power of demons and the power of Christ. Demon-possession is in itself a remarkable and terrifying demonstration of supernatural power. Now in the New Testament we observe not only a contrast between the malevolent activity of the demons and the beneficent work of Christ, but equally we see a contrast between the power of the demons and the omnipotence of Christ. There is contest and triumph.[4] The power of the demons is great and fearful, but it is seen to be totally subject to the authority of Christ. He 'gagged' the demon with one word ('Be muzzled'). He quelled every tempest, physical, mental and spiritual which demonic agencies had brought about. The wild beasts of darkness and shame released their prey at His command. His word was a word of infinite power and absolute authority.

An intriguing aspect of the knowledge which the demons have of Christ is seen in the fact that they are commanded to keep silent about it. It is almost as if there were a double secret, the private knowledge possessed by demons and the instruction not to divulge this secret. We

4. This reaches its climax in the conflict between Christ and Satan, as illustrated in the Temptation (Mark 1:13). Stonehouse observes that 'His conflict with Satan serves . . . to provide a background for the delineation of the struggle between the Son of God and the forces of Satan which is so prominent in the narrative of his ministry.' *The Witness of Matthew and Mark to Christ*, 21. The Tyndale Press, 1944.

see this very clearly in Mark's Gospel (1:34; 3:11, 12). The people are astonished at Christ's works, but the demons, possessing more than human insight, cry 'Thou art the Son of God'. As N. B. Stonehouse puts it, 'The Messiahship of Jesus, transcending purely human categories, could be perceived only on the basis of a supernatural discernment.' This insight was already possessed by demons, and an even greater insight could be given to men by the Holy Spirit. Christ commanded the demons to be silent, but permitted those whom He healed to witness to His power. To one such He said, 'Go home to thy friends, and tell them how great things the Lord hath done for thee, and hath had compassion on thee' (Mark 5:19). This the man did. Christ refused to allow the demons to bear witness to His Messiahship because, as Stonehouse well says, He would not permit 'the kingdom of Satan to be the agent of his revelation to men'.[5]

The power of Christ over demons must be viewed in relation to His total victory over Satan. Christ distinguishes between entering the strong man's house and binding him, on the one hand, and the spoiling of his goods on the other (Matt 12:29). The one secures the possibility of the other. The context of this statement in Matthew makes it clear that the spoiling of goods includes the casting out of demons. The demons are subject to Satan, and if Christ is to cast them out, He must first overwhelm their master. Geerhardus Vos effectively disposes of the view that Matthew 12:29 merely refers to Christ's own victory over evil, as experienced in the Temptation, before attacking it outwardly in the lives of others. The verse speaks of an objective struggle, and

5. Ibid., 57, 59.

does so in language much too strong to describe a merely subjective conflict.

The Jews were as much amazed by the manner in which Christ cast out demons as by the fact itself. By 'a word', 'with the finger of God', 'by the Spirit of God', He drove out the tormentors. All this was in marked contrast to the elaborate and not always successful ritual of their own exorcisms, with their many incantations and potions. Christ expelled the demons with a word, and invariably that word was obeyed. While Christ's public ministry was marked throughout by submission and even passivity, time and again there burst forth such a manifestation of divine power against the forces of darkness that the Kingdom of God unmistakably came to incipient realization in the days of His flesh.[6]

Christ and Exorcism:

We have already noted that exorcism was an established practice amongst the Jews when Christ came into the world. He referred to the practice on one occasion and said, 'If I by Beelzebub cast out demons, by whom do your sons cast them out? therefore shall they be your judges' (Matt 12:27; Luke 11:19). The Jews claimed that their exorcisms had divine sanction, but when Christ expelled demons in a manner utterly different from and incomparably superior to their exorcisms, they blasphemously accused Him of doing so by the power of Satan, thus perversely contrasting Christ's mode of healing the possessed with their own superstitious exorcisms.[7]

6. See Stonehouse, Ibid., 250.
7. Josephus describes Jewish exorcism in his *Antiquities*, viii, 2.5.

In Acts 19:14 we read of the abortive attempts of the sons of Sceva, who practised exorcism, to expel a demon. They did so ostensibly in the name of Christ, not because they were Christians, but because they had seen the apostle Paul casting out demons in that name. 'They took it upon them', we read, 'to call over them which had evil spirits the name of the Lord Jesus, saying, We adjure you by Jesus whom Paul preacheth.' However they soon discovered that the name of Jesus was no magic word. The demon answered, 'I recognize Jesus, and I know about Paul, but who are you?' Then the possessed man attacked the exorcists with such ferocity and power that 'they fled out of that house naked and wounded'. F. F. Bruce remarks that when these men tried to use the name of Jesus, 'like an unfamiliar weapon wrongly handled it exploded in their hands.' Not only were the charlatans discredited, 'the name of the Lord Jesus was magnified', and a great fear fell upon the people of Ephesus. The name of the Saviour was not to be trifled with, and the mighty works of the apostles were not to be imitated. The practitioners of magic had taken a beating and the result was that many who had dabbled in occult practices, 'curious arts' (Acts 19:19), brought their 'books' or magical parchments and publicly burned them. Several of such magical scrolls have survived to our day and may be seen in certain University libraries and museums. F. F. Bruce tells us that 'the special connection of Ephesus with magic is reflected in the use of the term "Ephesian scripts" for such magical scrolls', and he describes the spells which they contain as 'the merest gibberish, a rigmarole of words and names considered to be unusually potent, arranged sometimes in patterns which were part of the essence of the spell, but they fetched high prices.'[8] We read in Acts that this collection was worth 'fifty thousand pieces of silver'. The powers of darkness were worsted, and the Word of God 'mightily grew . . . and prevailed'.

Pagan exorcisms are simply a trick by which Satan brings people increasingly under his power. The stronger demon in the sorcerer will most certainly expel the demon in a possessed person. But that person is not healed. He has not been delivered from the power of the enemy. The expelled demon can and probably will return. The servant of Christ must not try to be a mere exorcist, for the simple reason that he wants to see the possessed person delivered once and for ever from the power of Satan. Our Lord has clearly condemned the practice of an exorcism which, by its failure to give the sufferer immunity from future demon possession, demonstrates its unsatisfactory character.

Our Lord's discourse on the theme of the departure from a man and subsequent return of an evil spirit (Matt. 12:43–45; Luke 11:24–26) is highly significant, particularly because of the guidance it affords to the missionary in seeking to find answers to the burning questions that arise from his experience of a culture infiltrated and dominated by demonic powers. For here is an apologue describing a 'cure' wrought by ordinary exorcism, and its main thrust is that to combat Satan apart from Christ is really to work for Satan and against God. The situation described would be familiar to the Jews. The exorcist has plied his art; the demon has departed and the victim is quite normal again. The life is now said to be 'swept and garnished'. But it is vacant; it has no occupier; the house remains without a resident.

8. Ibid., 389ff.

The person delivered is liable to be re-possessed at any moment. Indeed the demon has not been dispossessed. He can say, 'I will return unto *my house*.' Here lies the great weakness and indeed the uselessness of mere exorcism. Christ clearly shows that the empty life is in constant peril. There is no such thing as a spiritual vacuum. The exorcized spirit goes 'through dry places'—perhaps an expression from some Jewish formula of exorcism— remains unsatisfied and then resolves to return to his house, this time taking with him 'seven other spirits more wicked than himself'. This time the intention is to 'dwell there'. The word translated 'dwell' indicates permanent residence and is repeatedly used in this sense in Luke's writings. Now the last state of the man is worse than the first. The fact that our Lord applies this apologue to the Jewish nation (Matt 12:45) in no way reduces its relevance to our present study. Its teaching is of crucial importance. The main lesson is that before there can be permanent *dispossession* of a demon there must be a spiritual *repossession* of the victim. We know from the rest of Scripture that this can only take place through the new birth, as a result of which the person is indwelt by the Holy Spirit.

Some have seen demon-possession as an ugly caricature of what it means to be indwelt by the Holy Spirit. Certainly His indwelling is in sharp contrast to demon possession in that His gracious presence and influence enhance the human personality, enabling the saved man to glorify God and fulfil the purpose of his creation, whereas demon-possession unmans its subject, reducing him to a hollow, shameful travesty of what man was meant to be.

A closer look at the expulsion of demons during our

Lord's ministry and that of His apostles shows that such deliverance always took place in an evangelistic context. It was never divorced from the preaching of the Gospel.

The command to the Twelve to 'cast out demons' (Matt 10:8) is part of a wider command which begins with the words, 'As ye go, *preach* . . .' We have already noted that the expression 'What a word is this!' (Luke 4:36) refers to the preaching of our Lord and is not to be limited to His word of command addressed to the demon. The miracles of our Lord were never divorced from His teaching in general and there is no reason to think that He ever cast out demons without at the same time preaching the kingdom of God. Indeed He deliberately links the two. 'If I with the finger of God cast out demons, no doubt the kingdom of God is come upon you' (Luke 11:20). Having condemned a superficial act of exorcism as worse than useless, He certainly would not resort to such a practice Himself. Christ came to save men. The Christian worker confronted by the challenge of the powers of darkness must grasp the fact that men are not saved by an exorcism that leaves the citadel of man's being unoccupied. But if men are saved then much more than exorcism will have taken place. Men who are truly regenerated by the Spirit and Word of God are indwelt by God's Spirit and sealed by His Spirit unto the day of redemption (Eph. 4:30); neither principalities nor powers can separate them from the love of God which is in Christ Jesus our Lord.

The ministry of 'the seventy' (Luke 10:1ff.) in which demons were expelled, was essentially and primarily a ministry of the Gospel attended by the Holy Spirit. The demonic forces had to withdraw before that ministry, and, referring to it, Christ said that He saw Satan falling like lightning from heaven (Luke 10:17, 18). Similarly the casting out of demons during the ministry of the apostles was clearly associated with their preaching of the Gospel. Men were delivered from Satan when they became Christians.

This is well illustrated in the Book of Acts. It was as Philip preached Christ in Samaria that many were delivered from unclean spirits and that Simon the Sorcerer, or Simon Magus, as he is usually called, found himself outstripped and finally exposed for what he was. Like Balaam of old, he came to acknowledge the manifest power of God and considered it politic to serve this God. Bar-Jesus, the sorcerer of Paphos in Cyprus (Acts 13:6ff.), who did his utmost to prevent the proconsul Sergius Paulus from believing the truth preached by Paul, was sternly rebuked by the apostle who called him 'a son of the devil' and brought divine judgment upon him in the form of temporary blindness. Thus an evil influence was removed and the proconsul 'believed, being astonished at the doctrine of the Lord'. In all such cases the preached Word was triumphant and the powers of darkness were forced to retreat. The opponents of the Gospel mentioned by Paul in his second letter to Timothy (3:6–9) and classed with Jannes and Jambres (two of the Egyptian magicians who plied their arts against Moses), may well have practised magic after the style of the sons of Sceva and Simon Magus. Paul is confident that like Moses' opponents, these challengers of Christianity would be vanquished; and he urges Timothy to persevere in his calling as a minister of the Gospel (2 Tim 4:1ff). In the face of such diabolical opposition Timothy is enjoined to 'preach the Word'.

The apostles were not seeking to establish reformed

lives, 'swept and garnished', for they knew that such lives were not saved lives. They sought to preach the Word of God so that by that incorruptible seed men might be born again. The New Testament knows nothing of un-converted men from whom demons had been cast out by our Lord or His apostles. It never separates the preached Word from the results of that preaching. Whether Christ speaks directly to the demon, or uses the mouthpiece of the preacher, His word is still a word of power, and the finger of God is mighty to put the enemy to flight.

8

DEMONIC ACTIVITY SINCE
NEW TESTAMENT TIMES

Christian doctrine is founded on Scripture alone. It is a confession in faith of what is revealed in the Bible. But while the Church's creed is based on Scripture, it is confirmed in experience. The teaching of Scripture concerning continuing demonic activity is no abstract doctrine. It is uniformly endorsed by the testimony of the Christian Church.

The Church Fathers frequently referred to demon-possession and deliverance from it. When all vagaries and excesses have been removed from their writings on the subject, there still remains a firm core of belief in the reality of possession, and their warnings against occult practices are emphatic. In the *Didache*, a church manual of the late first or early second century, we read: 'My child, be no dealer in omens, since it leads to idolatry, nor an enchanter nor an astrologer nor a magician, neither be willing to look at them; for from all these things idolatry is engendered.'[1] In Augustine's *The City of God* there are many references to demons, demon-worship, necromancy and the influence of demons in the lives of men. In his refutation of Porphyry and 'his friends the theurgists' (supernatural magic), Augustine writes:

'Why, then, O philosopher, do you still fear to speak freely against the powers which are inimical both to true

1. *The Apostolic Fathers*, J. B. Lightfoot, Baker Book House, 1956.

virtue and to the gifts of the true God? Already you have discriminated between the angels who proclaim God's will, and those who visit theurgists, drawn down by I know not what art . . . Are not these the evil spirits who were bound over by the incantations of an envious man, that they should not grant purity of soul to another . . .? Do you still doubt whether these are wicked demons, or do you perhaps feign ignorance, that you may not give offence to the theurgists who have allured you by their secret rites, and have taught you, as a mighty boon, these insane and pernicious devilries?.'[2]

Justin Martyr (c. 100–163) deals with the subject of demon-possession in his first and second *Apology*, and the practice of adjuring demons in the name of Christ. He expresses the view that a demon would possibly obey, if adjured by a Jew in the name of the God of Abraham, of Isaac and of Jacob.[3] Often the demonology of the Fathers was extremely fanciful, but there can be no doubt concerning their firm conviction of the reality of possession; the office of exorcist was established quite early in the history of Christianity, especially with the development of episcopacy. 'The exorcists', according to Kurtz, 'took spiritual charge of those who were possessed . . . over whom they made the prescribed prayers and uttered formulae of exorcism.'[4]

2. *The City of God*, Vol. I, 418ff., T & T Clark, 1872. Compare Augustine's refutation of the view that the apostle Peter practised magic arts. Ibid., Vol. II, 289ff.

3. *The First Apology of Justin Martyr*, with notes by Bishop John Kaye, Griffith, Farran, Browne & Co.

4. *History of the Christian Church*, Vol. I, 113, T & T Clark, 1880.

Luther's Demonology:

Because, at the time of the Reformation, so much of Satan's work stood revealed, it is too often supposed that in pre-Reformation times demonic activity was less evident. But the reverse is the case. With the powerful revival of the Gospel, superstitions which, through Satanic influence, had gripped mediæval society, were greatly restrained. Commenting on this fact Luther writes, 'When I was a child there were many witches, which bewitched both cattle and men, especially children. But now these things be not so commonly heard of, for the Gospel thrusteth the devil out of his seat.'[5] The Puritan divine, Increase Mather, writes more fully on the same point:

'Some hath propounded it as a question worthy the inquiring into: What should be the reason that demons did ordinarily infest the Gentiles of old, as also the East and West Indians of later times, and that popish countries are still commonly and grievously molested by them; but in England and Scotland, and in the United Provinces, and in all lands where the Reformed religion hath taken place, such things are more rare. Popish authors do acknowledge that as to matter of fact it is really thus; and the reason which some of them assign for it is, that the devils are so sure of their interest in heretical nations, as that they pass over them, and come and molest Papists, whom they are most afraid of losing. But they should rather have attributed it to the light of the Gospel, and the power of Christ going along therewith. Justin Martyr, Tertullian, and others, observe that upon the first promulgation of the Gospel, those dia-

5. *Commentary on Galatians* 5:19.

bolical oracles, whereby Satan had miserably deceived the nations, were silenced; in which respect the word of Christ, Luke 10, 17, was wonderfully fulfilled. The like may be said as to Protestant being less imposed upon than popish nations by deceitful demons.'[6]

Though demonic activity was thus curtailed by the Reformation the Reformers had no hesitation over the fact that there is a continuing activity of demons in the affairs of men. Luther has much to say on the subject and at times appears even to be obsessed by it, attributing too many mishaps to demonic interference. He believed that there were demons infesting 'woods, water, swamps, and deserted places', and he felt that the demons generally were 'every moment . . . plotting against our life and welfare, but the angels prevent them from harming us'.[7] But Luther was not as morbid in his thinking about demonic activity as some would suggest. When a pastor came to him from Suptitz near Torgau, complaining of poltergeists, and saying that Satan hurled pots and dishes at his head, Luther answered, 'Let Satan play with the pots. Meanwhile pray to God with your wife and children and say, 'Be off, Satan! I'm lord in this house, not you. By divine authority I'm head of this household, and I have a call from heaven to be pastor of this church.'[8]

In 1535 Bernard Wurzelmann, pastor of the church in Dinkelsbuhl, wrote to Luther about a woman believed to be demon-possessed. Luther replied: 'The first thing you and your congregation ought to do is this: Pray fervently and oppose Satan with your faith, no matter

6. *Remarkable Providences*, 1856 reprint, 144.
7. *Table Talk*, 172, *Luther's Works*, Fortress Press, 1967.
8. Ibid., 280.

how stubbornly he resists. About ten years ago we had an experience of a very wicked demon, but we succeeded in subduing him by perseverance and by unceasing prayer and unquestioning faith. The same will happen among you if you continue in Christ's name to despise that derisive and arrogant spirit and do not cease praying. By this means I have restrained many similar spirits in different places, for the prayer of the Church prevails at last. Consequently you should have no doubt, if you pray in truth and with perseverance, that this wicked spirit will be humbled.'[9]

The following year a pastor in Frankfurt on the Oder wrote to Luther to ask advice concerning the treatment of a girl believed to be possessed. Her name was Matzke Fischer, and she had a long history of mental illness. Suddenly she became worse. A Roman priest tried in vain to exorcize the demon. 'We must', wrote Luther, 'persevere in our prayer for the girl and our contempt of the Devil until finally, Christ permitting, he lets her alone.' In both the above cases Luther urged that a thorough investigation be made to ensure that deception was not being practised. As he put it, 'I have encountered such frauds, and afterwards I reproached myself for my simplicity.'[10] So in spite of a rather fanciful demonology, Luther was remarkably sane in his advice, laying the main emphasis on prayer and faith, and the preached Word. 'The Devil', he wrote, 'hates the Word of God more than any other thing.'[11]

Luther's greatest contribution to the Church's policy in

9. *Letters of Spiritual Counsel*, 42, S.C.M. Press, 1955.

10. Ibid., 43.

11. Comment on Psalm 94:6, *Luther's Works*, Fortress Press, 1958.

dealing with this problem, was his great emphasis on the need for and the place of prayer in facing this expression of Satan's hostility. 'We cannot', he says, 'expel demons with certain ceremonies and words, as Jesus Christ, the prophets, and the apostles did. All we can do is in the name of Jesus Christ to pray the Lord God, of His infinite mercy, to deliver the possessed persons. And if our prayer is offered up in full faith, we are assured by Christ Himself (Jn 16:23), that it will be efficacious, and overcome all the Devil's resistance. I might mention many instances of this. But we cannot of ourselves expel the evil spirits, nor must we even attempt it.'[12]

The Conviction of Calvin:

Calvin's statements on Satan and on the activities of the demons are a model for all theologians to follow. His masterly treatment of the subject in his *Institutes* is always faithful to Scripture. He himself witnessed what he regarded as a definite example of demon-possession, and he tells of this in one of his letters. The man lived on the Ager Tugurium and Calvin described him as 'a wicked, worthless creature, known all his life long as a drunken, dissipated blasphemer', who came to a tragic end. But the Reformer was distressed by the fact that many members of the Council of Geneva 'were making a jest of the whole affair'. In the face of continuing scepticism Calvin cried, 'If you believe that there is a devil, you have here a manifest instance of his power. Those who believe not in God deserve to be blind in the midst of light.' Immediately after the strange and fearful end of

12. *Table Talk*, Hazlitt's translation, 267, David Bogue, 1868.

this man, Calvin preached on the matter to the Council. 'I went indeed so far as to say that, during these two days, I should have preferred death twenty times over, having seen those unfeeling countenances, could I have them witness the judgments of God. The ungodliness of our people was more than ever discovered by this affair. Few only agreed with us. I know not if even one really believed us from the heart.'[13]

Calvin's demonology avoided the acceptance of popular superstitions which appeared in Luther's, while their basic attitudes to demon-possession were alike related to the teaching of God's Word. Exorcism at baptism, as practised by Rome, Calvin forbade.[14] Instead he emphasized the need to be clad in the whole armour of God in the conflict with demonic forces, prayer and faith being all-important. He was deeply conscious of the hosts of wickedness arrayed against Christians, and saw them committed to an irreconcilable struggle.[15] It is clear from his commentaries that Calvin believed in demon-possession as a present reality. Rejecting the error that 'every man is attacked by his own particular devil', Calvin says, 'On the contrary, Scripture plainly declares that, just as it pleases God, one devil is sometimes sent to punish a whole nation, and at other times many devils are permitted to punish one man ... There is the greater necessity for keeping diligent watch, lest so great a multitude of enemies should take us by surprise.'[16]

This general position of the Reformers is reflected in

13. See *The Life and Times of John Calvin*, Paul Henry, Vol. I, 311, Whittaker & Co., 1849.
14. *Institutes*, Book 4, Chap. 15, 19.
15. Ibid., Book 1, Chap. 14, 13ff.
16. Comment on Mark 5:9.

the Confessions of the 16th century. The Second Helvetic Confession, 1566, speaks of Satan in the language of our Lord in John 8:44 and refers to the angels that fell of their own free will and who have become 'enemies of all good and of the faithful'. Referring to 'the apparition of spirits', it terms this a deception of the devil, and continues, 'In the Old Testament the Lord forbade the seeking of the truth from the dead, and any sort of commerce with spirits' (Deut. 18:11).[17]

Demonology and 'Witchcraft' in the 17th Century:

The English literature of the 17th century reveals both the penetrating and discriminating treatment of Satan's works in the practical writings of many of the Puritans and the crude delusions which remained popular among all ranks of society. Archbishop Cranmer's Articles of Visitation of 1548 had required every parish officer to discover 'any that use charms, sorcery, enchantments, witchcraft, or any like craft invented by the devil'.[18] Nevertheless these practices were so entrenched in England and Scotland that they survived as late as the 18th century. Fertility rites were also associated with the witch-cult, the important assemblies or 'Sabbaths' taking place at Candlemas (Feb. 2nd), May-eve (known later as Roodmas), Lammas (Aug. 1st), and November-eve (All Hallow E'en). Smaller and more frequent meetings known as 'covens' were held; the number in such local groups was always thirteen.

17. *Reformed Confessions of the Sixteenth Century*, Edited by Arthur C. Cochrane, S.C.M. Press, 1966.
18. Cranmer's *Works* (*Remains and Letters*), 158, Parker Society, 1846.

Undoubtedly the two leading Puritan observers of demonology, Cotton Mather and Increase Mather, were not sufficiently cautious in their acceptance of the supernatural, but their credulity was small compared with that of the majority of their day. It is not surprising that the common people were too often obsessed with the subject of witchcraft when even King James I wished to parade his learning on the subject, including the belief that the devil can teach his disciples how to draw *triangular* circles as a potent spell!

An epidemic of interest in 'witchcraft' was followed by an epidemic of harsh suppression in which many undoubtedly innocent of the alleged sin were put to death.

One of the most deplorable of episodes concerned the Salem Witchcraft trials in Massachusetts, in 1692. As the hysteria spread rapidly, hundreds were arrested and tried. Nineteen were hanged. Nevius records that the judges were burdened with a sense of the solemnity of the occasion and of personal responsibility. Judge Hale 'prayed the God of heaven to direct their hearts in the weighty thing they had in hand; for, to condemn the innocent, and let the guilty go free, were both an abomination to the Lord'. One by one the 'bewitched' appeared, and their personal testimony was decisive. If the 'bewitched' was thrown into 'fits' before the court, this was regarded as evidence of witchcraft. Sometimes those in 'fits' would accuse others in the district of witchcraft, and this was accepted as evidence.

Some have put the whole thing down to fraud, and have regarded the 'afflicted' as cunning actors who deceived the judges. But this, as Nevius remarks, 'is to suppose that a few ignorant children were able for months together to deceive the wisest heads of New

England; and that in that age intellectual ability was at its maximum in childhood, and diminished with increasing age'. Clearly some other explanation must be found. It is significant that despite their hallucinations and hysteria, the sufferers evinced remarkable consistency under examination, and even conscientiousness, preferring to die than perjure themselves. When asked in court how their 'tortures' were caused, they answered in several cases that they were caused by the Devil. Nevius agrees with this explanation, regarding the 'sufferers' as in fact demon-possessed, but not necessarily 'witches' or sorcerers. The judges, misled by the view of witchcraft so common in their day, instead of seeing the innocent accused as afflicted by evil spirits, regarded them as the instruments of such spirits. This seems to have been their cardinal and tragic mistake. To accept the testimony of the 'bewitched' regarding other people was a serious mistake. Nevius well says, 'Had the courts of Salem proceeded on the Scriptural presumption that the testimony of those under the control of evil spirits would, in the nature of the case, be false, such a thing as the Salem tragedy would never have been known.'[19]

19th-Century writers such as William Ross who speak of 17th-Century witchcraft provide valuable information, but they tend to treat it all as the product of superstitious ignorance. 'Perhaps', comments Ross, 'in a century or two others will look back with as great surprise on the table-turnings and spiritualistic professions of this age, as we do on the witchcraft of the seventeenth century'.[20] In other words, all the world needs is progressive en-

19. Ibid., 303ff.
20. *Glimpses of Pastoral Work in The Covenanting Times*, 206, James Nisbet & Co., 1877.

lightenment to dispel all suspicions of the supernatural! Similarly, Samuel G. Drake, in his *Memoir of Cotton Mather* written in 1852, comments thus on Mather's account of witchcraft given in his *Wonders of the Invisible World*, 1692:

'Many have reproached Dr Mather as though he was the author of that dismal and awful delusion. This is singularly unjust. He was himself one of the deluded. All the world then believed in witchcraft, and people entered into it according to their temperament and circumstances. The delusion was not a native of New England, but an exotic from the father-land; and it had been well if this had been the only one imported thence. Even when prosecutions had ceased, there was not a cessation of a belief in the reality of witchcraft; its progress was stayed from a very different cause, as is now too well known to be entered into or explained. Even to the present day there are thousands who believe in its reality; and that belief can only be extirpated by the progress of genuine knowledge. Within the remembrance of the writer, one might ride from Boston, in a single day, with a very moderate horse, into a New England town where the belief in witchcraft was very general.'[21]

The truth is that the demonic evil which caused the fear of witchcraft in the seventeenth century, with all its attendant excesses, is still with us. Beneath the legends and silly stories one can detect a substratum of reality. Behind all the smoke of superstition and ignorance there burned a fire of diabolical malevolence.

21. *Magnalia Christi Americana*, 1852 edition, vol. 1, xxxii.

John Wesley and the 18th-Century Revivals:

In touching upon the 18th Century we confine ourselves to the writings of John Wesley. No doubt at times
Wesley was too ready to see demonic influence, but that
he encountered it often during his remarkable lifetime is
scarcely open to dispute. Probably an event which
occurred when he was thirteen years of age accounts in
part for his life-long interest in the subject of the supernatural. On December 2nd, 1716, a strange disturbance
took place at Epworth Rectory, the home of his childhood. On that occasion, and subsequently, the household
was kept in a state of alarm by unaccountable groans and
knockings. Wesley's sisters named the disturber 'Old
Jeffrey' after a former rector. The 'ghost' would imitate
the Rev. Samuel Wesley's knock at the gate, and grow
boisterous when he prayed for the king. This state of
affairs lasted for several months, and then, with a few
exceptions, ceased. When John Wesley next visited
Epworth, in 1720, he spent some time gathering information which he published many years later. In August
1726 he copied other details from his father's diary. The
lively Hetty Wesley has been blamed for the disturbances,
but in view of thorough investigations at the time, the
suggestion is not convincing. Emilia Wesley claimed to
have received visits from 'Old Jeffrey' in 1750 at West
Street, London. And in the early nineteenth century a
rector of Epworth was driven to the Continent, with his
family, by the strange noises in the house.[22]

22. *The Life of John Wesley*, John Telford, 31, 360, Robert
Culley, 1886. *Memoirs of the Wesley Family*, Adam Clark,
245–291. *Life of Wesley*, Robert Southey, 16–19, London
1876. (See Appendix A – correspondence and conversation
among the Wesley family about the supernatural disturbances.)

Of the 'ghost of Epworth', Dr Adam Clarke wrote, 'The eye and ear-witnesses were persons of strong understandings, and well-cultivated minds, untinctured by superstition, and in some instances rather sceptically inclined.'[23] John Wesley himself was convinced that the noises were supernatural.

More important than the above is the record given by Wesley of incidents which took place after the beginning of the great revival in 1739. He tells, for example, of John Haydon, a respectable person who 'fell off his chair and began screaming terribly, and beating himself against the ground ... Two or three men were holding him as well as they could.' Confessing his sin in having declared Wesley to be a deceiver, the man then 'roared out, O thou devil! thou cursed devil! yea, thou legion of devils! thou canst not stay! Christ will cast thee out.' There were further physical reactions such as the heaving of the breast and profuse perspiration; and then, as others prayed, his torment passed and Wesley records that 'both his body and soul were set at liberty'.[24]

Another case was that of a young woman in Kingswood: 'I found her on the bed, two or three persons holding her. It was a terrible sight. Anguish, horror and despair, above all description, appeared in her pale face. The thousand distortions of her whole body showed how the dogs of hell were gnawing her heart. The shrieks intermixed were scarce to be endured. But her stony eyes could not weep. She screamed out ... "I am damned, damned, lost for ever. Six days ago you might have helped me. But it is past. I am the devil's now. I have

23. See *Memoirs of the Wesley Family*, Adam Clarke, 2nd ed., I., 246.
24. *Wesley's Journal*, entry for May 2nd, 1739.

given myself to him. His I am. Him I must serve. With him I must go to hell" . . . She then began praying to the devil.' Wesley tells that even this poor soul finally found peace.[25] Other cases recorded by Wesley included 'gnashing of teeth', 'roaring aloud', 'exceptional physical strength', 'horrid laughter', 'blasphemy grievous to hear', and the demon speaking through the possessed person, as in the case of N. Roberts in Bristol. Sensing what Wesley terms 'a preternatural agent', a friend present asked, 'How didst thou dare to enter into a Christian?' and received the reply, 'She is not a Christian. She is mine.'[26]

All his life Wesley was firmly convinced of the reality of demon-possession. Replying to a certain William Black, one of his missionaries in Nova Scotia, who wrote to him about certain demoniacs, one of them particularly virulent, Wesley commented: 'It is well that Satan is constrained to show himself so plainly in the case of these poor demoniacs. Thereby he weakens his own kingdom, and excites us to assault him more zealously.'[27] At Stratford-upon-Avon in 1743, Wesley ministered to a woman whose physical convulsions and bellowings were particularly horrible and who had been declared a demoniac. He did not question this opinion, and as he prayed, he was conscious of preternatural feelings and of the tremendous crisis through which the woman was passing.[28]

It must, however, be added in connection with

25. Ibid., entry for October 23, 1739.

26. Ibid., Obtober 25, 1739.

27. *The Life and Times of John Wesley*, Vol. 3, 541, L. Tyerman, London, 1870.

28. Quoted by Robert Southey, Ibid., 365.

Wesley's testimony, that even in his long ministry clear cases of demon-possession were rare and it is apparent that some occurrences amidst scenes of emotional excitement require no supernatural explanation. There were instances of feigned distress, as Charles Wesley reports in telling of a girl at Kingswood who 'confesses that her fits and cryings out ... were all feigned that Mr Wesley might take notice of her'.[29] And he also speaks of 'many counterfeits' including self-induced physical phenomena.[30]

From the accounts of the revivals of the 18th Century it is apparent that Satan was generally at work in ways other than demon-possession. By encouraging hysteria and fanaticism, and by mimicking the work of the Spirit so as to bring evangelical religion into disrepute, he sought to confuse and hinder the cause of the gospel. As Jonathan Edwards wisely observed in his book *The Religious Affections*: 'There are other spirits who have influences on the minds of men besides the Holy Ghost. We are directed not to believe every spirit, but to try the spirits whether they be of God. There are many false spirits, exceeding busy with men, who often transform themselves into angels of light, and do in many wonderful ways, with great subtlety and power, mimic the operations of the Spirit of God.'[31]

The Ulster Revival of 1859:

During this revival there was a reappearance of the physical phenomena already noted in the Methodist awakening of the previous century. One observer, the

29. *Journal of Charles Wesley*, August 5, 1740.
30. Ibid., June 4, 1743.
31. *The Religious Affections*, Jonathan Edwards, 69, Banner of Truth, 1961.

Reverend J. M. Killen wrote: 'With regard to physical manifestations, I may mention that some of these were very violent . . . comparable to nothing I have ever read of, save the demoniacal possessions in the New Testament. I have seen, for instance, four strong men quite unable to hold or restrain a young lad of about eighteen years of age; and I have known parties of this type, after the paroxysm had ceased, left so weak for a little that life appeared to be almost extinct – reminding me of the individual mentioned in Mark 9:26, of whom it is said, that when the unclean spirit "cried and rent him sore, and came out of him, he was as one dead" '.[32]

At a service in County Cavan on 1st October, 1859, attended by about 1500 people, a wild cry suddenly interrupted the preacher's voice, and was soon taken up by hundreds more. The affected were removed and soon over 300 people were lying in the church, or in the manse, or among trees near by. Reverend Thomas Y. Killen gives the following detailed description of some of the 'strikings'. 'One class of cases we had, resembled, more than anything else I can think of, the demoniacal possessions in our Lord's day. The whole bodies of the persons affected were convulsed in the most frightful manner, so that it required five or six strong men to hold them, while their cries were of the most piercing kind. These frightful cases were comparatively few in number, and I regret to say, have not generally turned out well. Several of those who passed through fearful struggles have gone back to their old ways, and instead of getting better, seem rather to have grown worse.'[33] Killen then relates several

32. *The Year of Grace*, a History of the Ulster Revival of 1859, William Gibson, 173, Andrew Elliot, 1860.
33. Gibson, Ibid., 363.

instances which bore all the marks of the demoniac.

Because such incidents as these appear to have been occasioned by revivals it is erroneous to conclude that we would be better without revivals. Certainly there is more danger of fanatical excess in times of revival but, as Spurgeon says, 'I had sooner risk the dangers of a tornado of religious excitement than see the air grow stagnant with a dead formality'.[34] 'Many things occur', writes George Smeaton, 'which all too plainly prove that it is necessary not only to pray for an awakening, but for wisdom equal to the occasion when it is imparted'.[35]

Demon-Possession in 19th-Century China:

Some striking cases of demon-possession in China during the 19th century have been recorded. John L. Nevius went to China as a missionary in 1854, with a strong conviction that a belief in demons belonged to a barbarous and superstitious age. He listened with a tolerant scepticism to the many stories about demon-possession and the power of the sorcerers. In vain he tried to convince the people to whom he spoke that their views were the result of ignorance and imagination. But soon he began to doubt his own scepticism. Eventually he was completely convinced that demons did exist and that demon-possession was a terrible reality. In his book, *Demon Possession and Allied Themes* he gives a number of instances of possession which he witnessed, and many others recorded for him by reliable pastors and missionaries. Among the cases which he recorded was that of a

34. *An All-Round Ministry*, 173, Banner of Truth, 1960.
35. *The Doctrine of the Holy Spirit*, 251, Banner of Truth, 1958.

woman named Kwo. When he met her she was thirty-two years of age and had suffered from possession for eight years. Her friends brought her to Leng, a Chinese servant of the Lord, begging him to cast out the spirit. They had done their best to do so and had failed. 'I have no power to do anything of myself', answered Leng: 'We must ask God to help us.' As they prayed the woman was lying on an earthen bed (common in North China), apparently unconscious. When they had finished praying she was sitting up, her eyes closed, with a fluttering of the eyelids and her hands tightly clenched. Leng addressed the demons: 'Have you no fear of God? Why do you come here to afflict this woman?' He received this reply: 'God and Christ will not interfere. I have been here seven or eight years; and I claim this as my resting-place. You cannot get rid of me'. Similar utterances followed with great rapidity. 'I want a resting-place, and I'll not leave this one.' She was dragged away, her condition unchanged. Some months later Leng was present at a church two miles away from where Mrs Kwo lived. The Christians were praying for her. Mrs Kwo herself was in the company of Christians in her own village, also assembled for worship. Demon-possessed, she was determined to prevent the service taking place. Raving wildly she threw Bibles and books on the floor. She was joined in this behaviour by another woman, and as they raved together, they were heard to say to each other: 'Those three men are coming here, and have got as far as the stream.' When asked, 'Who are coming?', the answer was given with great emphasis, 'One of them is that man Leng'. As Leng was not expected to visit that village for several days, a member of the family said to the raving woman, 'He will not be here today.' To which the demon replied: 'If he does not come here today, then I am no *shien* (spirit). They are now crossing the stream, and will reach here when the sun is about so high,' and she pointed to the west. When Leng and his companions arrived on the scene they rebuked the demon, which continued to say, by the woman's mouth, 'I'll not go! I'll stay and be the death of this woman!' But as prayer continued a great calm came over the two women who seemed to have awakened as if from sleep. Mrs Kwo stepped forward with all the charm and courtesy of her race and made the visitors welcome. Soon she gave evidence of faith in Christ and was later baptized by Nevius in company with another minister named Leyenberger. Nevius wrote: 'As far as I know she has had no return of her malady.'[36]

Equally impressive are the instances of possession recorded by Pastor Hsi, the Confucian scholar who became a Christian, that of his own wife being, perhaps, the most notable. Shortly after his conversion to Christianity, Hsi noticed a change coming over his wife. Although well in body and mind, she became moody, restless and scarcely able to eat or sleep. She was tormented by suggestions of evil. At the time for daily worship she was full of ungovernable rage. Soon all the signs of possession were present, great violence, terrible language and physical convulsions that resembled epilepsy. The neighbours linked this visitation with Hsi's conversion. He had, they said, turned to doctrines of evil spirits and was reaping his reward. Hsi cast himself on God, fasting and praying for three days and nights. Obviously God answered the prayers of His servant, for the demons were repulsed and Mrs Hsi was not only delivered but

36. Ibid., 30ff.

declared herself to be a Christian and so she became one with her husband in his life-work. She never again suffered in this way. In Christ she was delivered from the power of Satan. Her deliverance caused a great stir in the district. 'Who can this Jesus be?' asked many, and some followed her example and turned to the Saviour.[37]

The twentieth century, too, affords its examples of demon-possession, alas! all too numerous. Robert Petersen witnessed the case of Mrs Lo, during missionary labours in Indonesian Borneo.[38] When he first saw her, six men were trying to restrain her. Her strength was superhuman. Occasionally she would break away from the six pairs of hands holding her. Her invective was shocking to hear. A Chinese herbalist gave her tranquillizers and finally she boarded the bus on which Petersen was also to travel. Throughout the journey she continued to rave. The missionary prayed silently for her. Later, in the providence of God, she was brought to the Petersens. They prayed and for the first time Mrs Lo listened to the Gospel. 'It's true', she said, 'I know it's true, my heart tells me it's true.' Her heart was prepared by the Holy Spirit to receive the Word and she believed in Jesus Christ as her Saviour on that very first hearing. Her deliverance was complete. The means used by God were prayer and the preaching of His Word.

Agreement of Evidence:

The evidence of demon-possession and kindred phenomena, supplied by missionaries for many generations now, remains remarkably consistent irrespective of

37. Ibid., 68ff.
38. Ibid., 86ff.

their geographical location. Among the common marks of possession which they list appear the following:

(1) Speaking in a voice not that of the victim.

(2) Unusual physical strength.

(3) Obvious conflict within the person.

(4) Hostility and fear in the presence of Christ when proclaimed in His Word.

(5) Greatly heightened insight and sensitivity.

(6) Speaking in tongues.

(7) In cases of involuntary possession the same physical and mental disturbances as are described in the New Testament are observed.

(8) Voluntary possession, as with sorcerers and spiritist mediums, is often employed to effect healing, sometimes with phenomenal results.

Evangelical missionaries are convinced of the reality of demon-possession today, and find it one of their greatest challenges and problems.[39]

39. For other examples of apparent demonic activity within the framework of religion, and especially in times of revival, see the writings of John Cennick, fellow-worker with John Wesley, and Arthur Fawcett's account of the Cambuslang Revival in Scotland in the 18th Century. (*The Cambuslang Revival*, Banner of Truth, 1971.)

9

DEMON-POSSESSION AND
THE AUTHORITY OF SCRIPTURE

C. H. Spurgeon reminds us that 'the turning-point of the battle between those who hold "the faith once delivered to the saints", and their opponents, lies in the true and real inspiration of the Holy Scriptures. This is the Thermopylae of Christendom.'[1] The battle between supernaturalism and naturalism has several fronts, but the crucial area of conflict concerns the nature of the Bible. Is the Bible the inspired (God-breathed) record of divine revelation, completely trustworthy and our only standard of belief and conduct? or is it an imperfect, human document through which God speaks existentially to man, the experience of man being the final reference point of all meaning? A man's answer to that question will determine his philosophy and his theology. B. B. Warfield declares: 'The real question, in a word, is not a new question but the perennial old question, whether the basis of our doctrine is to be what the Bible teaches, or what men teach.'[2]

Those who accept, in faith, the Scriptures as the inerrant Word of God, and who submit to its authority, have no difficulty in believing in the existence of demons and in the reality of demon-possession. They have accepted the supernatural in the very first sentence of the

1. Spurgeon's Preface to L. Gaussen's *Theopneustia*, 4th edition, Chas. J. Thynne, 1912.

2. *The Inspiration and Authority of the Bible*. 226. Presbyterian and Reformed Publishing Company, 1948.

Bible. They believe in this God. He is their Saviour. They believe whatever He tells them in His holy Word. Those who approach the Bible from a humanist and rationalistic standpoint, submit the Bible to their own judgment and this attitude immediately excludes an acceptance of the supernatural as revealed in Scripture. This is theological modernism.

Theological Modernism and Demon-possession:

The 'liberal' theologian discounts the Biblical account of demonic activity. In his view, angels, whether fallen or unfallen, including the Devil, belong to the realm of myth and reflect an outside and pagan influence on the writers of Scripture. This opinion finds popular expression in commentaries and sermons. In his Commentary on Mark, C. Leslie Mitton writes:

'Today we are not accustomed to speak of "evil spirits" or "demons", as men of ancient times did. Nevertheless we still suffer from the same ills as those which they attribute to the malicious presence of such spirits, ills that wreck human happiness, and sometimes jeopardize life itself. Such ills are fear, guilt, remorse, shame, resentment, jealousy, hate, depression. Or we may give to them psychological names, such as neurasthenia, neurosis, psychosis and so on. These names perhaps suggest how difficult to control these emotional disturbances can be, and how man can feel himself utterly dominated by some evil power before which he is helpless. By whatever name we call them, these evil spirits are subject unto Jesus and to the healing power He still brings to human life.'

Commenting on a demon's address to Christ (Mark

1:24), Mitton says, 'The first one to recognize Jesus is a man of abnormal mind. Such people do sometimes show uncanny perception.' With reference to the temptation of Christ the same writer remarks, 'Perhaps we today speak more easily of the "power of evil" than of a personal Devil, but Jesus certainly spoke of "Satan".'[3] This is a fairly typical statement of the liberal attitude to the subject.

Emil Brunner speaks for theological liberalism in general when he writes: 'For the Fundamentalist, of course, this subject presents no particular problems. The Bible speaks of angels and of devils; in accordance with the Scriptures therefore, we can do so too. But for us *this* way is impossible.' Brunner then proceeds to state that 'our final authority is not what Scripture says, but its relation to the centre of Christian Faith as a whole, that is, the will of God made known to us in Jesus Christ'. Admittedly, he says, the Bible speaks of angels and spirits, good and evil, 'but it really tells us very little' and 'what it does say is not at all instructive, and it presents no uniform view.' 'It is impossible', says Brunner, 'to formulate a doctrine of angels and spirits . . . without arbitrary unification and expansion of the text of the Bible.'[4] Brunner, and those who think like him, replace personal spirits with impersonal 'demonic' forces, and when they speak of the 'demonic' and 'the Satanic' they mean something wholly different from what the writers of Scripture meant when they wrote about angels, demons and spirits. They will, at times, even apply the personal pronoun to the Devil, but viewed in

3. *The Gospel According to St. Mark*, The Epworth Press, 1957.

4. *Dogmatics*, Vol. II, 133ff., Lutterworth Press, 1952.

the context of their theology as a whole, this can only be regarded as allegorical language on their part.

Another example of the liberal interpretation of the teaching of Scripture concerning evil spirits is found in William Neil's exposition of Hebrews 2:14. He sees the picture of Christ victorious over Satan as fairly common in the New Testament and describes it as 'one which would strike a chord in minds familiar with the mythology of the Graeco-Roman world where gods came down to earth to do battle for men. The fact that the Hellenistic mind would see it as a fairy-tale come true is no less reason for the early Church using familiar pagan concepts to communicate Christian truth, than for preaching the gospel to Jews in the equally mythological framework of Satan and his myrmidons. The basic truth for Jew and Gentile, and for us, is that through Christ death is swallowed up in victory.'[5] In sum, the theological modernist will affirm with Brunner: 'We must be ready to admit that even the Biblical writers were children of their own day and that the world from which they derived their ideas has no authority for our faith.'[6]

The liberal theologian professes high regard for the will of God made known to us in Jesus Christ. Yet it is precisely at this point that the liberal and not the conservative is in difficulty. Christ's conflict with Satan and demons was a major part of His earthly ministry, and it is clear that the existence and wickedness of Satan were much in His mind. He had come to destroy the works of the devil. It is obvious from the Gospels that He believed in the objective reality of demons and in the

5. *The Epistle to the Hebrews*, S.C.M. Press, 1955.
6. Ibid., 147.

fact of demon-possession. If we accept the liberal inter-pretation of demonology and regard it as mythical and of pagan origin – 'possession' being merely the way that primitive peoples explained baffling diseases – then the veracity of Christ is immediately at stake. Several theories have been proposed in order to account for this problem.

(1) *The non-involvement theory:* On this view Christ purposely did not correct the popular opinion of His day, considering that it was not necessary for Him to do so and not wishing to engage in a controversy which was not relevant to His essential ministry. But we have already seen that the conflict with the powers of evil lay at the very heart of Christ's mission. On this view, Christ allowed the people to remain in ignorance for the sake of avoiding controversy and offending deep-seated prejudices! It is inconceivable that the Lord should so act and yet claim to be the Light of the world!

(2) *The accommodation theory:* It is said that our Lord merely used current language in much the same way as we use a term like 'lunacy'. By using that term we do not imply any belief that the moon (Latin, *luna*) has caused certain mental illnesses, although in the distant past such a belief was held. It is quite obvious that our Lord's attitude to demons and possession was utterly different from this. Plainly He conveyed the impression that He believed in the existence of demons and their activity. Indeed He even made it part of His disciples' commission to 'cast out demons'. This theory leaves us with a Saviour who accommodated Himself to current opinion and terminology to such an extent as to utter what was un-true; and, like the previous theory, presents a Jesus who

[133]

was not even honest. How else could we describe some-
one who spoke of demons entering a man if in fact He did
not believe in the existence of demons at all?

(3) *The limitation theory:* This is the fairly common
view that Christ shared the contemporary belief in the
existence of demons and therefore His Word is not final
for us. It is claimed, for example, that His attitude to the
Old Testament and to the universe was simply that of a
first-century Jew. This view leaves us with a Jesus who
shared the superstitions and limitations of His day. It at
least has the merit of presenting a sincere Jesus, but the
fact remains that it presents a Jesus who was often
sincerely wrong. But if Christ is unreliable when He
speaks about Satan and demons, when *is* He reliable, and
why? It is impossible for us ever to regard such a person
as the King of Truth.

(4) *The refraction theory:* It is asserted that Christ did
not cast out demons, but that the Evangelists have
erroneously attributed this to Him. They could only
describe, it is said, the healing power of Christ on the
bodies and minds of men in language intelligible to
themselves and to their age, and so they gave a 'refracted'
account, that is an account coloured by their own culture
and outlook. This theory only transfers the problem from
the veracity of Christ to the veracity of Scripture. Alfred
Plummer puts it neatly when he says, 'If the demons
were there, and Christ expelled them and set their
victims free, there is nothing to explain: the narrative is
in harmony with the facts.'[7] It needs to be stressed that
the Gospels consistently and repeatedly present Christ as
healing demoniacs and putting the demons to flight.

7. *Commentary on Luke*, 136. International Critical Commentary, T & T Clark, 1896.

The first two theories impugn the veracity of Christ; the third presents a merely human Jesus and the fourth impugns the veracity of Holy Scripture. All four views are inconsistent with a belief in the full Deity of Christ. The anti-supernaturalism of modernist theology may pay its hollow tribute to God's revelation in Jesus Christ, but it really worships a Jesus of human reconstruction and not the Christ to whom the Scriptures bear witness and which contain His saving truth for our souls.

William Barclay boldly states the viewpoint of anti-supernaturalism when he writes: 'Either, He knew no more on this matter than the people of His day, and that is a thing we can easily accept, for Jesus was not a scientist and did not come to teach science, or, He knew perfectly well that He could never cure the man in trouble unless He assumed the reality of the disease. It was real to the man and had to be treated as real or it could never be cured at all.' Thus we are given a choice of limitation or accommodation. To Dr Barclay it does not matter whether or not we believe in the reality of demons. 'The point is that the people in New Testament times did.' He concludes his comments on Mark 1:23–28 thus: 'In the end we come to the conclusion that there are some answers that we do not know.'[8] So far as demonology is concerned nothing is gained by rejecting the answer which God has given us in His Word. The Jesus and the Bible of the theological modernist quite evidently are not the Jesus and the Bible of the evangelical, and consequently on this as on all other doctrinal and ethical subjects, we come to conclusions which are not only divergent but which are diametrically opposed. For

8. *The Gospel of Mark*, 24–28, The Saint Andrew Press, 1956.

as J. G. Machen pointed out, modernist theology and orthodox Christianity are really two quite different religions.[9]

As theological modernism swept through the Church over a century ago, in deference to the prevailing philosophical and scientific climate of the day, belief in the supernatural was regarded as an old, mediaeval relic. Modern churchmen were in the vanguard of those intellectuals who 'laid' the supernatural. Modern man, it was argued, could not be expected to believe in spirits in a world in which the wonders and triumphs of science increased almost daily. Philosophy, logic and psychiatry had all the answers. To ask twentieth-century man to accept Biblical dogmas was an insult to his intelligence. The Bible must be 'demythologized.'

All seemed to be going well until modern man became difficult. In an age in which the tenets of humanism were more consistently applied than at any previous time, there occurred what is now termed the 'occult explosion'. The spiritual nature of man cannot be suppressed indefinitely, and frequently it will express itself in the most bizarre fashion accompanied with the strangest aberrations. Liberal churchmen suddenly found themselves out of fashion in a day when ouija boards, séances, witches' covens and exorcisms became quite common and stole the headlines in newspapers and periodicals. Embarrassed churchmen spoke unconvincingly in televised interviews. At the same time a number of their colleagues urged a return to exorcism in the old mediaeval style.

Some years ago the Church of England decided to

9. *Christianity and Liberalism*, 2. The Macmillan Company, 1923.

appoint diocesan advisers on exorcism in a number of cities, and in 1972 the Report of a Commission on Exorcism, convened by the Bishop of Exeter, was published.[10] Contributors to this Report included two members of the Society of Jesus and a member of the Benedictine Order. Not surprisingly the emphasis is strongly sacerdotal and even magical; indeed the Report speaks of 'sacerdotal exorcism'. Consequently in the section of the Report which sets forth liturgical practice, we find repeated references to the sprinkling of holy water, the sign of the cross and the observance of the Lord's Supper. In fact the recommended liturgy is typical of the mediaeval exorcisms practised by the Roman Catholic Church. The Papacy has had its exorcists for centuries. Such exorcism, which lays all the emphasis on ecclesiastical ritual and forms, may produce results, just as other forms of exorcism produce results. But the pragmatic test will not suffice. Mere exorcism, as we have seen, finds no support in Scripture and stands condemned by it. Nothing less than actual salvation can meet the need of any sinner. Nothing less than the preached Word will, in normal circumstances, effect deliverance and renewal.[11]

The recent book by John Richards, *But Deliver Us from Evil*, is an important and scholarly contribution to the present discussion of this subject.[12] Richards is an

10. S.P.C.K., 1972.

11. By the use of the term 'normal circumstances' we distinguish between the salvation of responsible adults and that of infants and of the mentally deficient.

12. Other significant books written on Demonology, during the past century or so, include the works of W. M. Alexander, (T & T Clark. 1902), J. L. Nevius, T. K. Oesterreich (*Possession*

Anglican and for nine years served as secretary of the Bishop of Exeter's Study Group on Exorcism. His book contains a wealth of valuable information and represents many years of intensive study. He is primarily concerned with the demonic dimension in pastoral care and what is termed 'deliverance ministry'. He makes it plain that he is not interested, in this particular book, in establishing a demonology as such. Here, in the opinion of this writer, lies his main weakness. His approach is pragmatic and ritualistic rather than Biblical and Reformed. The Scriptures are not really regarded as normative, but simply as supplying valuable evidence along with a great deal of other valuable evidence. Richards sees himself providing the 'raw stuff' from which theology must be 'hammered out'. 'That', he says, 'is the theologians' job, not mine,' and he calls for 'a theological readjustment to accommodate the facts' which he presents.[13]

Richards fails to see the weakness of this pragmatic approach. Whose 'facts' are we to accommodate? Those of his book, or those of Christian Science, or Spiritism, or what? Because of his failure to recognize Scripture as the sole norm by which all facts are to be interpreted, Richards finds room for belief in 'earth-bound spirits', that is, departed loved ones who are earth-bound by past sins, guilt or trouble and who need the service of the Church to release them; and also for prayers for the dead and visitations from the departed. He quotes J. B. Phillips' account of two alleged visits to him by the late C. S. Lewis.[14] In all such writing we search in vain for

Demoniacal and Other, Paul, Trench & Trubner. 1930). Of these Nevius' work stands closest to the Scriptures.

13. Ibid., 219.

14. *Ring of Truth*, 89, Hodder & Stoughton, 1967.

conversion in the Biblical sense: the approach is decidedly non-evangelical.

Conservative Theology and Demon-possession:

The majority of orthodox Christians believe in demon-possession as a continuing phenomenon in human experience, but not all. Some, like R. L. Dabney, express a reverent agnosticism on the subject. Dabney, says: 'Whether "possessions" occur now, I do not feel qualified to affirm or deny.'[15] Others believe that demon-possession was confined to the time of our Lord's earthly ministry or that its occurrence outside that period is extremely rare. If that be so, then what passes for possession today may largely be accounted for in psychological and pathological terms, and the sincerely held opinion of hundreds of missionaries in many parts of the world is mistaken. It should also follow that what has been considered as possession may be successfully treated, or at least alleviated, by psychiatric and neuropathological methods. To this last point we shall return, but first of all we must consider the attempt to find Biblical warrant for the view that demon-possession was either entirely or almost entirely restricted to the days of Christ's earthly ministry.

One of the first writers to propound this theory was the learned Dr William Menzies Alexander, whose controversial book, *Demonic Possession in the New Testament*, is often cited as an authority on the subject. Alexander combines medical and theological knowledge in his treatment of the subject, but at times his handling of Scripture betrays an approach bordering on rationalism,

15. Lectures in Systematic Theology, 274, Zondervan Publishing House, 1972.

and while there is much valuable material in his work, it needs to be read with discrimination. We discuss his book here because it has been influential, in one particular respect, in conservative circles. Alexander makes the criterion of possession 'the confession of Jesus as the Messiah or Son of God', and he then applies this criterion consistently in his examination of the Biblical data. This leads him to the conclusion that there are no cases of genuine demonic possession apart from the earlier portion of our Lord's ministry. He then uses much ink in an examination of the early documents of the sub-apostolic age and the writings of the Church Fathers, finding many references to demon-possession which he regards as bearing all the marks of 'ethnic demonology' and of pagan views which had invaded the Church. Alexander traces his subject through mediaeval and on to modern times, noting particularly the work of J. L. Nevius. The examples of possession given by Nevius are dismissed as cases of epileptic insanity or some other mental disorder.

Alexander's thesis is that 'the incarnation initiated the establishment of the kingdom of heaven upon earth. That determined a counter-movement among the powers of darkness. Genuine demonic possession was one of its manifestations.' This phenomenon was, according to Alexander, 'unique in the history of the world, being confined indeed to the earlier portion of the ministry of our Lord.' Strangely enough, he agrees that King Saul was demon-possessed. His view that the essential criterion of possession is a confession of Jesus either as Messiah or the Son of God is inconclusive. It does not follow that the demoniac's confession of the Deity of Christ, when in His immediate presence, presupposes such a confession to be an essential sign of possession. Alexander fails to take into account the testimony of missionaries in modern times, that people who are said to be possessed, but who have never heard the Gospel, have, in the presence of missionaries, revealed a certain knowledge of Christ. Indeed Nevius, whose conclusions Alexander peremptorily discounts, gives a remarkable example of this. Alexander fails to prove his assertion that 'according to the evidence of the Gospels, these demonic testimonies had their beginning and end in Him'. Our Lord was fully conversant with Jewish belief in demons, and while He rejected outright mere exorcism (Luke 11:24–26), there was obviously agreement between Him and His hearers concerning the reality of demon-possession. This conviction was firmly established among the Jews long before Christ came into the world, and He never questioned it. He did not teach them something which they already knew only too well, nor did He ever suggest that demon-possession was only a new phenomenon peculiarly associated with His appearance on earth. The Biblical evidence is decidedly against Alexander's thesis.

The bizarre theories and excesses of some of the Church Fathers in the field of demonology are quite irrelevant to the question before us. What is significant is that, despite excesses and mistakes and even the influence of ethnic demonology, the belief in demon-possession was firmly held. A belief so common to mankind demands an explanation. The fact that in its ethnic forms it is grotesque and degrading and vastly different from Biblical demonology is not the point here. The real question concerns the origin of so universal a belief among men. The rationalist will say that the age-old belief in spirits and demons is a superstitious invention with no basis in reality. But granted an original revelation of Divine truth and a common knowledge of that truth, it is just as reasonable to believe that despite all the distortions universal knowledge has descended from that original revelation.

The view of W. M. Alexander is repeated in a modified form by J. N. Geldenhuys in his excellent Commentary on Luke's Gospel. Geldenhuys does not try to establish any criterion of genuine demon-possession, but he is emphatic that 'demon-possession is a phenomenon which occurred almost exclusively, but then to be sure on an amazing scale, during Jesus' appearance on earth and to a lesser extent during the activity of the apostles'.[16] He sees possession now as comparatively rare, but believes that it will reappear at the end of the age and then Christ will finally triumph over the Evil One. Leon Morris holds a similar view and sees demon-possession as apparently 'a phenomenon especially associated with the earthly ministry of our Lord', to be interpreted as an 'outburst of demoniacal opposition to the work of Jesus'.[17]

While there may have been a great upsurge of demonic activity during our Lord's earthly ministry, it is by no means certain. It is just as arguable that the presence of the Light of the world exposed the activity of sinister forces preferring the cover of darkness, and when Christ by His word cast out demons, and the only remedy for this affliction was found, it naturally became a wonder of the time. Such a view is just as tenable, indeed more so, than that of Geldenhuys. It is fallacious to argue that because there seems to have been an intensification of demonic activity especially in the form of demon-possession, during our Lord's earthly ministry, that the same

16. See note on 'Demon-possession', p. 174 of his Commentary.
17. *The New Bible Dictionary*, 310, IVF 1962.

phenomena are now either non-existent or extremely rare. There is no hint in Scripture that Satan's forces would, in due course, be less vicious in their attacks on mankind than when Christ was on earth, and there is nothing in human experience to suggest such a relaxation on Satan's part. The advocates of this view have not given sufficient thought to the world-wide phenomena of spiritism or to the spirit which animates the heathen religions. Such a study does nothing to encourage the belief that demon-possession is largely a thing of the past. The spiritist medium, as we have seen, is the modern counterpart of the person described in the Old Testament as having a 'familiar spirit', and just as common!

The Jews of our Lord's day had their own elaborate theories of demons and exorcism.[18] From what source did they derive this acute awareness of demonic activity? There certainly is no evidence in the New Testament that 1st-Century Jews were suddenly confronted with new and unfamiliar phenomena; the contrary is the case. And on the view just noted, how do we account for their long established methods of exorcism, if possession were comparatively rare prior to the commencement of Christ's earthly ministry? Besides, the writings of Josephus and other ancient Jewish authors refer to the practice of exorcism.[19]

An attempt has been made on exegetical grounds to establish an eschatological case for believing that possession has now virtually ceased. The passages quoted are

18. Edersheim, ibid., Vol. I, 482 and Appendices 13 and 16.
19. It is interesting to note that Layard discovered bowls inscribed with forms of Jewish exorcism among the ruins of Babylon. *Helps to the Study of the Bible*, 281, Oxford University Press, 1931.

1 Timothy 4:1, 2 Thessalonians 2, Zechariah 13:2 and Revelation 12:13.[20] Paul's statement that 'in the latter times some shall depart from the faith, giving heed to seducing spirits, and doctrines of demons', is taken as a reference to demonic activity in the last days of the Old Testament era. But this passage is a clear prediction of imminent apostasy in which 'seducing spirits' would lead some to accept 'doctrines of demons'. E. K. Simpson states that the expression 'the latter times' seems to intimate 'a less distant future than the commoner phrase "the last days", occurring in 2 Timothy 3:1.' Simpson continues, 'It should be borne in mind that the apostle is not depicting contemporary phenomena, but heresies ere long to be hatched.'[21] It is indeed hard to see how 1 Timothy 4:1 can be put into reverse and referred to the closing days of the Old Testament era.

The passage in 2 Thessalonians 2 refers to the Man of Sin being hindered and restrained, and it is urged that when this is related to statements that Satan is 'bound' and 'bruised' we may conclude that such restraint necessarily involves the virtual cessation of demonic activity in the form of possession. Satan will, in the future, it is said, intensify his rage against the Church, redoubling his efforts, but in the meantime we live in a millennial era in which we no longer encounter demon-possession as a common contemporary phenomenon. But this is a deduction which lacks Biblical warrant. The picture in Revelation 12:13 of the dragon cast into the earth yet persecuting 'the woman which brought forth the man

20. See, for example, *The Big Umbrella*, Jay E. Adams, article entitled, 'Demon Possession and Counselling', Presbyterian and Reformed Publishing Company, 1972.

21. *The Pastoral Epistles*, 64, The Tyndale Press, 1954.

(child)', cannot be limited to a brief period during our Lord's earthly ministry, or to a season immediately before His second coming. Satan's malignant persecution of the Church has been his work throughout the centuries and in Revelation 12 we are shown his utter defeat.

In Zechariah 13:2, God states that there is a day coming when He 'will cut off the names of the idols out of the land, and they shall no more be remembered: and also I will cause the prophets and the unclean spirit to pass out of the land'. This passage is seen by some as a prediction of a time when the 'unclean spirits' would be removed. The translation of this verse given by H. C. Leupold is to be preferred: 'I will cut off the names of the idols out of the land, and they shall no more be remembered: and I shall also remove the prophets and the spirit of uncleanness out of the land.'[22] God says that He will banish three things: idolatry, false prophecy or the prophets who teach the cult of idol worship, and the spirit of uncleanness which animates and characterizes all false prophecy and idolatry. The passage has no bearing on the subject of demon-possession. It is a fact of history that after the Exile, Israel did abhor idolatry and it was banished from the land.

Some have sought to establish the theory of demon-possession being restricted to the time of Christ's ministry on earth because of practical problems in evangelistic counselling. Failure in counselling has sometimes been attributed to the presence of a demon, and much confusion and damage, for both counsellor and the person being counselled, has resulted from a hasty diagnosis of possession. This tends to shift responsibility from the person being counselled; for he is viewed as, and feels

22. *Exposition of Zechariah*, Baker Book House, 1965.

himself to be, a helpless victim to be pitied, rather than a guilty sinner who should repent. For those who react against this error it would be convenient if it could be established on a Biblical basis that in fact demon-possession has virtually ceased. But the problem remains only so long as the counsellor continues to think in terms of a possible exorcism. When he grasps the fact that he is not called upon to diagnose or decide whether or not the person is demon-possessed, but simply to proclaim the liberating word of Christ and proclaim the name of Christ,[23] the problem is gone. All who are saved by that name are set free from Satan's jurisdiction, and if that jurisdiction should happen to include demon-possession the individual concerned will also be delivered from that. There is no need to try to establish a strained eschatological escape route when faced with this problem. This is not to deny that at times the Lord's servant may feel reasonably certain that he is confronted by a 'possessed' person, nor to overlook the fact that in New Testament and also in modern times ordinary people have rightly sensed a demonic presence, but rather to emphasize that there is not one technique for 'ordinary' sinners and a special technique for 'demon-possessed' sinners. It is not the responsibility of the Christian worker to decide definitely that a person has or has not a demon. That is a knowledge possessed by his Master and in proclaiming His name the missionary or counsellor has obeyed his Lord. The outcome of all such proclamation is in the hands of a sovereign God.

23. See Chapter 11 under 'The Challenge to the Church's Method,' p. 164.

Psychology and Demon-possession:

Psychiatry and neuropathological treatment undoubtedly have their uses, but demon-possession and subjection to occultism are beyond their reach. Many psychiatrists adopt humanistic presuppositions when discussing this subject and consequently insist that demon-possession does not exist. A group of psychiatrists met in London a few years ago to hear an address on demonology. During the discussion which followed two psychiatrists insisted that possession simply did not exist. On their humanistic presuppositions it *could not* exist, therefore they dogmatically asserted that it did not. But two other psychiatrists rose to state that not only did they believe in the reality of possession, but that on several occasions they had, in their own practice, come across people whom they regarded as being possessed.

Psychiatry as such has no remedy for demon-possession. It may recognize and grapple with the psychological disturbances caused by possession, but it cannot remove that cause. If it assumes the non-existence of possession, it cannot offer deliverance. The malady is spiritual and the cure must be spiritual. A non-theistic psychology which obliterates all distinction between man and beast, and blurs the distinction between beast and the inorganic world, and which is wedded to a consistently evolutionary philosophy, assuming that the behaviour of animals sheds direct light on the behaviour of man, can only see man as something wholly different from what the Bible declares him to be.

It is sometimes asserted that in deciding whether or not demon-possession has any basis in fact we should be guided by the 'experts'. But *who* are the experts? Those who accept the Biblical doctrine of man and evil, or those who reject that doctrine? The latter are incapable of helping men and women who are enslaved and tormented by the Evil One, their very presuppositions precluding the possibility of touching those in need; but the former have witnessed the immediate deliverance of the demonically enslaved as they ministered to them the Word of Life. The minister of the Gospel, the Christian doctor of medicine and the Christian psychiatrist may all combine, in their respective spheres, to assist the person who has become entangled in spiritism and its occult allies.

It is important to emphasize that although the symptoms of epilepsy, insanity, melancholia and similar disorders are sometimes associated with demon-possession in the New Testament, these diseases are not in themselves to be traced to a demonic source. There is clearly a difference between mental illness and demon-possession, although Cornelius Van Til makes the theologically valid point that 'irrationality in the mind of man, that is, insanity, must be the result of a deflection of man from the source of absolute rationality', God, and consequently 'all men have merited insanity because of their departure from God'. Eternal punishment is 'the abyss of irrationalism', and 'what we call rational or normal experience is a gift of God's common grace. No man is worthy of it.'[24] This fact is far too often forgotten. Yet in practical terms there is a very definite distinction between mental illness and demon-possession. In the majority of cases of mental illness it is probably correct to say that the form of disorder is to be explained in medical terms. This may be

24. Syllabus, *Psychology of Religion*, 63, Westminster Theological Seminary, 1961.

true even of persons who believe that the Devil is responsible for their condition. Yet it must be recognized that in the field of mental and nervous diseases our knowledge is very limited. Some who have worked with mental patients testify that in certain rare cases of insanity there is a malignant hostility. Archbishop Trench wondered whether, if an apostle were to enter an institution for the insane, he might not 'recognize some of the sufferers there as "possessed"';[25] and Professor Rendle Short, a distinguished member of the medical profession in his day, and cautious in his approach to this subject, asked, 'What do we really know about the ultimate causes of mental disease, or even of epilepsy? ... Are we quite sure that no spiritual adversary has a hand in it, in some cases, if not in all.'?[26] Perhaps Short puts the question too strongly, but he does show the folly of a dogmatic rejection of the very idea of demon-possession by pseudo-science. With respect to epilepsy doctors distinguish between *symptomatic epilepsy* and *idiopathic epilepsy*. The former may be traced to a cause such as brain damage, a tumour or a liver disorder, to give a few examples. The latter cannot be traced to any known physical cause. It is reliably reported that two out of three epileptics in Britain and the United States suffer from idiopathic epilepsy.[27] How, then, on scientific grounds can psychiatrists object to the Christian's belief in the reality of demon-possession, when there are several such areas where science is in the dark? John Wilkinson, a member of the Royal College of Physicians and a trained theologian, writes, 'If demon possession is a fact

25. Ibid., 175.
26. *Modern Discovery and the Bible*, 126, London 1954.
27. John Richards, Ibid., 99.

there seems no reason why it could not be a cause of some cases of epilepsy.' He adds, 'Demon-possession is usually denied on dogmatic grounds, but it would seem much more dogmatically congruous to recognize the existence of demons and the possibility of possession.'[28]

The inadequacy of humanistic psychology to give help in the field of demonic activity may be illustrated by one example. In all instances recorded in the New Testament, deliverance from demon-possession, when it comes, is sudden. In cases recorded in more recent times deliverance occasionally has come through a protracted struggle lasting for several months; but even that is a comparatively quick way of being delivered from so terrible an affliction. On the other hand, it is common knowledge that the treatment of mental illness is a slow, tedious process. Supposing, as some suggest, that demon-possession is only a primitive way of accounting for a severe kind of mental derangement, then we would naturally expect any relief to be both slow and gradual. The opposite is true; and it is just as true that modern science has no adequate explanation for, and no real help to offer to, the person who is possessed.

Deceit is an essential weapon in Satan's armoury, and it needs to be remembered that he is not limited to the cruder forms of possession familiar among primitive peoples. The form of demonic activity best suited to further his ends in heathen lands might well have the opposite effect in nominally Christian societies. Demon-possession, especially voluntary possession, need not always express itself in crude and easily recognizable forms, and there is no reason to think that those who had

28. 'The Case of the Epileptic Boy', *The Expository Times*, LXXIX, No. 2.

'familiar spirits' in Old Testament times displayed the crude symptoms associated with the helpless victims of involuntary possession of whom we read in the New Testament. Doreen Irvine reports that present-day sorcerers are often highly respectable people who drive big cars and stay in the best hotels, yet their secret art is, beyond all question, of their father the Devil and has all the marks of a terrifyingly evil supernaturalism. The same may be said of the spiritists. Outwardly they may be like other people, but the atmosphere of the spiritist séance is charged with an evil presence and power. Even if ninety-five per cent of the happenings in spiritist meetings be explained in terms of trickery (the manipulation of light and sound, ventriloquism etc.,) and psychology (mental telepathy), there still remains a narrow but fearful margin of phenomena which cannot be explained by such means. They can be explained only if we allow for impersonating spirits, spirits who have convinced some of the greatest intellects of the 'truth' of 'spiritualism'![29]

Goethe was right when he wrote: 'People don't know the Devil is there! Even when he has them by the throat!'

29. For a study of spiritism see *The Chaos of Cults*, Pickering & Inglis, 1958.

10

CHRISTIANITY AND OCCULTISM

The word 'occult' comes from the Latin 'to hide' and so it refers to something secret, mysterious and beyond the range of ordinary knowledge. Today it is widely used with reference to magic and spiritist phenomena.

As we have seen, there are numerous references in the Old Testament to the evil supernaturalism practised in heathen lands, especially in the Egyptian and Babylonian courts. That ancient occultism, which completely dominated the pagan cultures of Old Testament times, persisted through the ages. It still dominates pagan cultures and is eroding a nominal Christianity, flourishing where irreligion is common. There is really nothing to choose between the gross forms of occultism in Old Testament days and those which are becoming increasingly common in our time. Behind all occultism there looms the sinister shape of spiritism. This is true whether we consider the popular spiritist healer in Brazil or the crude sorcerer of Borneo. It is this irruption of evil spirits which makes the practice of occultism so potentially dangerous.

The Current Obsession with Occultism:

Whenever man is cut off from fellowship with his Maker, whether by spiritual darkness and ignorance, or by wilful apostasy, he inevitably expresses his innate religious instinct in some perverse form. It is not surprising that in the present time, with much apostasy in the professing Church, and widespread materialism and resurgent humanism in society as a whole, we observe the spiritual nature of man finding devious and perverse forms of satisfaction. Lord Byron makes Satan say, 'He who bows not to Him (God) has bow'd to me.'[1]

Today there is a world-wide interest in the occult, and we hear much of black magic, white magic, spiritism, extra-sensory perception, exorcism and Satan-worship with its 'black masses' and other depravities. There has been a rush on the part of publishers, playwrights and film-producers to 'cash in' on the current craze and so to feed it. Books reveal the 'secrets' of the occult; novels are based on this tingling theme; plays often relate to spiritism; cinemas are crowded to see bizarre presentations of demon-possession and serious programmes on radio and television are devoted to a discussion of such phenomena. The interest is evident in schools where children experiment with ouija-boards and spiritist séances are not unknown. Other phenomena such as table-tapping and levitation of solid objects are by no means rare. The fascination and excitement of all this for young people is obvious. Often they dabble in these things out of curiosity. Ouija-boards have been listed in some toy catalogues! Probably the majority of those who first dabble in the occult do so for fun, just as horoscopes in the daily newspapers can be read merely for amusement. And the horoscope will depend upon which paper is read! Yet what begins as apparently innocent fun can soon assume a serious aspect. The regular reader of horoscopes is subconsciously influenced by what is read, and there is abundant evidence to show that the reading of these prognostications will have a subtle yet powerful

1. Cain: A Mystery, *Poetical Works* of Lord Byron, 525, Oxford University Press, 1959.

influence upon one's life. The results of dabbling in occultism can be both tragic and dangerous, as some have found out to their cost. Quite recently the British Press reported an instance where pupils at a school in England had been using ouija-boards 'for fun'. But things went badly wrong. Afterwards two of the boys kept going into trances and attacking their friends. One even tried to strangle another and later could not remember the attack.

The current interest in occultism is illustrated by the fact that in one region in Britain, if not more, the Post Office recently installed a 'dial-a-horoscope' service to its customers! John Richards tells that when 'The King of the Witches', Alex Sanders, was interviewed on television in Britain, the company concerned expected a large number of complaints; but the switchboards were jammed by people wanting his *help*! Richards also reports that Pan-American Airlines offer 'Psychic Tours of Britain' – complete with séance – to American tourists![2]

There is reliable evidence that 'witches' covens' are more plentiful than is generally realized. According to a recent newspaper report, a representative of the Church Army, who has made a special study of personal problems raised by occultism and black magic, stated that he knew of about twenty witches' covens in the Birmingham area alone.[3] A similar situation is said to exist in America and on the continent of Europe. Whatever reservations we may have about some aspects of Doreen Irvine's book, *From Witchcraft to Christ*,[4] there seems no doubt at all that she describes a world of occultism which is active in our day and which is the peculiar domain of evil spirits.

2. Ibid., 78 and 192.
3. *Daily Telgraph*, 26 Nov., 1973.
4. Concordia Press, 1973.

The Real Danger of Occultism:

Experiments in extra-sensory perception (E.S.P.), dabbling in horoscopes, palmistry, astrology and suchlike, may on the surface seem harmless and amusing. The 'reading' of cups, the use of Tarot cards, and all other forms of 'fortune-telling' are regarded by thousands as an innocent pastime. But this is only the circumference of the occult, the outer circle of the whirlpool. Step by step, and stage by stage, the more serious and frightening aspects of 'magic' are reached, and people then find themselves heavily involved in immorality, Satan-worship and demon-possession. A great deal of magic and occultism is so much nonsense and hocus-pocus, but it provides an easy entrance for demonic forces, and the warnings of Scripture against it should be heeded. The same is true of drug addiction, in that this experience can also become an entrance point for demonic forces. It is significant that drug addicts frequently show a keen interest in occultism, and that the taking of drugs at satanic gatherings has long been habitual. While it is true that the unregenerate person has no safeguard against the assaults of the Evil One, there is much greater danger when that person deliberately toys with the unknown powers of the occult. Any form of self-cultivated abandonment, physical or mental, is also highly dangerous. The attempt to render the mind vacant, or to project it into a world of unlimited fantasy is fraught with peril; and so is the submission of the human body to wild and uncontrolled expression, often coupled with the most primitive rhythms. The wild dances of some savage tribes in preparation for possession by the spirits, and the physical and mental phenomena which follow, are clear evidence of the danger of such abuse of mind and body. Christian young people especially should be suspicious of certain forms of 'pop' music which engender a wild and crude abandon which at best is undignified and at worst is suggestive of evil. Indeed some of this music is dedicated to sexual promiscuity and the use of drugs.

The Alternative to Occultism:

First of all there must be a firm belief in a personal God whose providence overrules our lives at every point. This will mean an experience of the reality of prayer and of guidance in daily living and important decisions. Occultism is a blatant and defiant denial of God. The person who believes in luck and 'lucky charms' and is generally superstitious, does not truly believe in the 'only true God'. A belief in a sovereign and gracious God whom we may know as our loving Father and Friend is the first and most important alternative to occultism.

Secondly, there is the acceptance of the Bible as our only rule of faith and practice. Without the Scriptures there can be no saving knowledge of God or of His will for us. As a man reads the Bible he may know his future in Christ or out of Christ, and that future is quite certain. The believer will turn his back upon the 'astrologers, the stargazers, the monthly prognosticators, (Isa 47:13), not to mention the daily prognosticators! Instead he will seek to know God's Word as a lamp unto his feet, and a light unto his path (Psa 119:105).

Thirdly, there is the daily practice of prayer as a means of communion with God. When the Bible is prayerfully read, and when prayer is governed by the Word, then fellowship with God becomes tremendously real and precious. In contrast the crystal balls and zodiacal signs of occultism are seen for the tawdry and evil trash they are.

Fourthly, we must maintain the fellowship which can only be found in Christ's Church. The worship of God in private, and corporately as we meet with His people, is a fellowship of light which is absolutely necessary if we are to serve God effectively in this world and be delivered from fellowships which are not of God.

These are the four main alternatives to occultism: belief in a personal God who has revealed Himself to us in Scripture and supremely in His Son, acceptance of His Divine Word as our sole guide in thought and action, daily communion with God in prayer, and the maintenance of fellowship within the Church of Christ.

Occultism is secret and hidden; it is dark and mysterious; it shuns the light. Ultimately, it leads to the vortex of demonism and Satan-worship. Even if the person who dabbles in it never sinks to that low level, he will still be blinded by superstition and will walk in darkness. If followed long enough, occultism can lead to character change, psychological illnesses and the development of mediumistic tendencies. Christianity, on the other hand, is open. It is God's revealed love and grace. It leads to light and life. It brings peace and assurance. Christianity is of God: occultism is of Satan.

Our present Duty:

There is the duty of example. Our whole life and bearing should testify to the fact that our God is real, and that He has given meaning and direction to our lives. We must show that we really believe in Him, that we have in Him as a fountain of living waters something infinitely better than the broken cisterns from which so many seek to quench their thirst.

There is the duty of influence. In our friendships, conversations and similar encounters in life, we should seek to witness directly to others, not being afraid to state our convictions. Frequently the opportunity to do so will present itself quite naturally. If we have won the respect and confidence of others, especially of our own age-group, they may well invite our opinion.

There is the duty of patience. When we meet those who are interested or even involved in occultism we must be careful to avoid being censorious and hypercritical. Interest in the occult usually implies that a person is not satisfied with material things. There is a thirst for something better. We must recognize that cry for help and meet it in sympathy and love. Occasionally we may meet the 'pusher', the hardened devotee of spiritism and occultism who seeks by every means at his disposal to involve others in his dark deeds. Here it is necessary to realize that we are faced with a deadly enemy and that 'we wrestle not against flesh and blood, but against spiritual wickedness (literally 'wicked spirits') in high places' (Eph 6:12). In that situation we must make sure that we are clad from head to foot in the armour described by Paul in Ephesians chapter 6, and that we use no other weapon save the Word of God, even as Christ Himself used no other weapon when confronted by Satan in person. John Bunyan in his vivid account of Christian's fight with Apollyon tells how he conquered the Dragon with the sword which had been given him:

A more unequal match can hardly be,
Christian must fight an angel; but you see

[158]

The valiant man by handling sword and shield,
Doth make him, tho' a dragon, quit the field.

The world of evil can be overthrown only by the Word and by the Spirit of God.

11

THE CHALLENGE OF THE DEMONS
TO THE CHURCH OF CHRIST

The true Church of Christ, guided by Scripture alone, knows that Satan and his forces remain active and that demonic activity will continue to the end of time. This belief, founded upon the Word of God, is confirmed in the experience of the Church in a world which makes Satan its god, accepting his word and rejecting that of the Lord God. The Church is profoundly aware of certain phenomena which can only adequately be explained if the belief in the reality of demon-possession is retained. Engaged in the 'work' of God, she is conscious of that 'counter-work' of which Satan is the undoubted author. The Church is also conscious of the subtlety and cunning of Satan, of his many arts and guises, of his masquerades and camouflage. The true Church dare not 'demythologize' the demons, for this would mean a rejection of Divine revelation and an arrogant assertion of man's ability to measure all phenomena by the measure of his own mind. The Church is challenged by the existence and continuing activity of the demons. She must be precise as to the exact nature of that challenge.

The Challenge to the Church's Faith:

Faith in the lordship of Christ gives fibre to the Church's service, and peace amidst every conflict. Belief in the triumph of Christ over Satan and all his forces is of paramount importance when from a purely human standpoint the enemy seems unconquered and unconquerable. The Christian Church must accept God's Word of victory in faith, and not be guided by her own observations. She must believe the Word of God against all odds. If at times there has been a missionary crisis, if the Church has faltered and lost heart, it is because of a lack of conviction of the lordship of Christ. A mere, formal confession of that lordship will not suffice in the heat of battle. An intellectual assent to a creed, however Biblical that creed may be, will not endure the onslaught of the foe. There must be a passionate conviction that Christ is Lord, a conviction which is wedded to a deep love of the Saviour and a daily communion with Him. Anything less must fail.

The Challenge to the Church's Obedience:

Christ has commissioned His Church to preach His Word and promised to be with her all the days. Through the preaching of that Word He accomplishes His purpose. It is the Church's privilege to obey her Lord and leave the outcome in His sovereign hand. Whether she be in the position of Noah in the midst of an unbelieving generation, or in the position of Jonah who witnessed a widespread belief of the Word he preached, she will rest content in the Divine assurance, 'My word . . . shall not return unto me void, but it shall accomplish that which I please, and it shall prosper in the thing whereto I sent it' (Isa 55:11). The Church will also bear in mind that the proclamation of the divine Word has a twofold result; it softens some and it hardens others. 'We are unto God a sweet savour of Christ, in them that are saved, and in them that perish: to the one we are the savour of death unto death; and to the other the savour of life unto

[161]

life . . .' (2 Cor 2:15, 16). The Gospel, as Calvin reminds us, 'is never preached in vain, but has invariably an effect, either for life, or for death' (*in loc.*). The sweet fragrance of the Gospel has a deathly smell to the impenitent and results in everlasting death.

A Gospel ministry is both awesome and demanding. Paul asks, 'Who is sufficient for these things?' Who can be the instrument of so momentous a task and shoulder a responsibility so stupendous as this? Paul quickly gives the answer: 'not that we are sufficient of ourselves, . . . our sufficiency is from God' (2 Cor 3:5). None but the men who see their own utter weakness can know and experience the sufficiency of God's grace. No self-sufficiency can cope with the demands of a ministry whose ultimate result is either the salvation or damnation of the hearers. This is not to overlook the fact that men are lost whether or not they hear the Gospel. The all-too-common assertion of many evangelists that men go to hell only for rejecting Christ, finds no support in Scripture. Where would men have gone if Christ Jesus had not come into the world? But the rejection of the Gospel confirms the sinner in his guilt and adds to his punishment (Matt 10:15; Luke 12:47, 48).

In humble trust and dependence upon God, it is the Church's wisdom to obey and to wait in hope. She must sow the seed that has been entrusted to her. The Harvester is God and the harvest is in His hands. Once this is forgotten, once it grows dim, there will be a tendency to doubt and fear, if not to panic.

The Challenge to the Church's Oneness:

Christian missionaries in such lands as Brazil, Ethiopia and Borneo, are frequently confronted by the challenge of Satan-worship and demon-possession, and by the exorcisms and healings which are practised by exorcists and spiritists. They are conscious of an evil and oppressive atmosphere. They are frequently deprived of the fellowship which they enjoyed in their local congregation in the homeland. Of necessity they must live in fairly close contact with one, two or more other missionaries, who might or might not be their chosen companions in normal circumstances. There is something abnormal about their way of life. They are different from the people around them. Simple actions can be easily misunderstood. In some areas the female missionary cannot even go for a walk alone. Loneliness, frustration, irritation, physical and mental exhaustion, all build up to oppress the spirit. Doubt assails. Fears arise. The gap between the 'theory' learned in Bible College days and the stern realities of the missionary situation suddenly seems very wide. The missionary battles on in prayer and faith, and with many tears. This is not to suggest that missionaries have no joy and peace, or that their experience is uniformly depressing. It is simply to recognize the reality of the situation as confided by missionaries again and again. It would be strange if it were otherwise. We would be puzzled if the messenger of Christ entered a veritable 'Satan's seat', confronted the 'depths of Satan' with the victory of Christ, and met with no opposition or temptation. But that is not the sole reason for the anguish experienced by many missionaries. Too often the church which has sent them forth, and of which they are a part, virtually for-

[163]

sakes them. Their salary is paid; their reports are received and circulated; here and there a faithful soul prays for them, and perhaps even writes to them. That is good, but it is not enough. The Church is one and she must strive to express that oneness in all she does. Nowhere is this more necessary than in her missionary outreach. The challenge of the demons to the small band of hard-pressed missionaries is a challenge to the whole Church to unite with them in earnest prayer and faith in the lordship of Jesus Christ. When this happens the missionaries will know, and the Church at large will be refreshed.

The Challenge to the Church's Method:

Awareness and concern in the face of sinister demonic phenomena, although commendable, must be wedded to sound method. There must be a theology of victory behind and beneath the Church's method of confronting Satan and his demons. Such method must be squarely based upon Biblical teaching, and must not be governed by any other considerations whatsoever. Here the principle of *sola scriptura* is of the utmost importance. Yet it is precisely this principle which has so often been forgotten. Well-meaning Christians frequently draw conclusions based on observations and then belatedly seek to buttress those conclusions with verses of Scripture which do not always support the preconceived beliefs.

There is always the temptation to follow the example of others and in doing so to lose sight of Scriptural teaching. The use of the name of Jesus in seeking to effect deliverance from demon-possession comes to mind. In some Christian circles there is an attitude to the name of

Jesus which almost borders on magic. It is believed that the very sound of that name will terrify the demons. It did not do so in the case of the seven sons of Sceva (Acts 19:13f.) Or it is believed that it is sufficient to command a demon in the name of Jesus to withdraw and thus exorcise the spirit. Appeals are made to certain portions of Scripture which are said to authorize such a procedure. This is to overlook the Biblical use of the word 'name'. It is never a mere label in Scripture. On the contrary it is an expression of the nature and character of the one who bears it. God's name reveals Him as an eternal Being and He expounds His name as He reveals Himself to His people. And so God's name is said to be 'declared' (Psa 22:22), 'proclaimed' (Ex 33:19), 'published' (Deut 32:3), and it is the 'help' of His people (Psa 124:8). It is 'a strong tower: the righteous runneth into it and is safe' (Prov. 18:10). In the New Testament, the name of Jesus is used in a similar fashion. Christ's name stands for His character and teaching. To proclaim His name is to tell forth the truth concerning His Person and work. Philip, for example, preached 'the things concerning the kingdom of God, and the name of Jesus Christ' (Acts 8:12). Paul confessed that before his conversion he acted 'contrary to the name of Jesus of Nazareth' (Acts 26:9).

Well-meaning Christian workers, jealous for the glory of their Master, sometimes feel that they should follow the practice of commanding demons in the name of Jesus to depart. But if there is no experience of salvation through the preached Word, what has been accomplished? In attempting mere exorcism, some searching questions need to be asked: What is the *source* of such a 'deliverance'? What has been done that the sorcerers could not do? Was the name of Jesus ever meant to be used for merely medical and therapeutic purposes? The whole weight of Biblical evidence is solidly against such a practice, for it can only be regarded as fraught with the gravest peril for all concerned.

The 'great signs and wonders', the exorcism of demons, the 'many wonderful works' which our Lord and the apostles associate with Satan and his dupes, are still to be witnessed. They are facts which cannot be denied, and frequently the name of Jesus is associated with them. There have been remarkable healing campaigns where the preaching was marked by the wildest doctrinal aberrations. The 'results' seem impressive and the evangelical, losing sight of his Biblical standards and un-wittingly accepting worldly standards of success, is in grave danger of what Martyn Lloyd-Jones calls 'capitula-tion to phenomena'. This is the error of allowing one's doctrine to be determined by phenomena. The facts cannot be gainsaid, so it is decided that they must be accommodated by theology and therefore theology is adjusted accordingly. But it is not necessary to do this. On the contrary, the Christian should seek to interpret the facts in the light of the teaching of Scripture. He must not allow phenomena to determine his belief. In warning against this peril, Martyn Lloyd-Jones remarks:

'People have assumed, because the name of Christ has been used in a meeting, that all that happens in it must be truly Christian, and is, therefore, a guarantee of the soundness of all that is taught. For them the results guarantee everything. I have known good people who, because of something they have seen in "healing meet-ings", have abandoned what they formerly believed. Because of what happened in a given meeting they have submitted to the entire teaching of those conducting that meeting'[1]

In other words, they have capitulated to phenomena. They have allowed facts to determine their faith, instead of interpreting facts in the light of their faith. They reach conclusions on non-Biblical grounds. They have totally failed to heed our Lord's warning in Matthew 7:22-23 and the apostle's warning in 2 Corinthians 11:13-15. Christ spoke of many who would say to Him, in the judgment, 'Lord, Lord, have we not prophesied *in thy name*? and *in thy name have cast out demons*? and *in thy name* done many wonderful works?' His reply is solemn and sobering: 'And then will I profess unto them, I never knew you: depart from me, ye that work iniquity.' So Satan can and does use the name of Jesus to do mighty works, including the exorcising of demons, in order to deceive men and gain greater power over them. As the apostle tells us, he appears as an 'angel of light' and the 'false apostles' employed by him are transformed 'into the apostles of Christ' and 'ministers of righteousness'. Christians need to pay heed to these words; they are intended to guide us and to protect us from impostors. In making this point we are in no way denying the power of God to heal the sick, if it be His will to do so. Our sole concern is to warn against a gullible acceptance of all phenomena associated with the name of Jesus Christ, especially where the exorcism of demons is concerned. All Christian workers, wherever they are called to labour, must remember that the outcome of their service for the Lord is in His sovereign hand. His purpose of grace will not fail. 'I have sworn by myself, the word is gone out of

1. *The Supernatural in Medicine*, 30, Christian Medical Fellowship pamphlet, 1971.

my mouth in righteousness, and shall not return, That unto me every knee shall bow, every tongue shall swear' (Isa 45:23). Once the Christian worker loses sight of the sovereignty of God, once he allows the sovereignty of electing grace to slip into the background and forgets that the same Gospel which is 'the savour of life unto life' to some is 'the savour of death unto death' to others, then he is in danger of becoming depressed in mind, mistaken in belief and misguided in action.

The greatest weapon which the Church possesses is the Word of God proclaimed in the fulness of His Spirit. Here are the *facts*, and no fact is truly understood when divorced from the Divine revelation of Holy Scripture. The Gospel unfolded in Scripture is said to be the 'power of God unto salvation' (Rom 1:16), and here the word translated 'power' (dunamis) is the word from which our English word 'dynamite' is derived. When we face Satan with the sword of the Spirit, we do so with the weapon he dreads most. Our Lord in His temptation used no other weapon. Let the Lord's people unite to rely in faith and obedience upon the sole mighty Word of God, and God will give peace to them, blessing their efforts in accordance with His sovereign purpose of grace, and using the prayerful proclamation of that Word to bring about the ultimate doom of the adversary.

The Challenge to the Church's Spirituality:

Is it not a fact that all too often, perhaps more often than not, the Church at large lacks the fervour and power experienced by believers at Pentecost? The risen Lord said to His disciples, 'Ye shall receive power, after that the Holy Ghost is come upon you' (Acts 1:8). This power was to be wholly different from what the world terms power. Instead of the political power which once they had sought, they would receive heavenly power. The command was, 'Tarry ye in the city of Jerusalem, until ye be endued with power from on high' (Luke 24:49). At Pentecost the Holy Spirit came to believers in a new fashion and inaugurated a new era in the life of the Church. We read that 'they were all filled with the Holy Spirit' (Acts 2:4). And we are commanded to be so filled (Eph 5:18) so that we may know the 'power' of Pentecost. It is true that Pentecost, as the commencement of a new era, was a once-for-all event. That glorious dawning does not need to be repeated, but we certainly need to walk in the light of that day. Too often believers 'grieve the Spirit' (Eph 4:30) and 'quench the Spirit' (1 Thess 5:19), instead of being 'filled with the Spirit'. Too often in the present century the picture of the Church is to be found in the letters to the Seven Churches in Revelation, chapters two and three. The power of Pentecost is sadly lacking, because the Holy Spirit is not honoured and loved.

If conservative theologians produce a reactionary theology in the face of modern Pentecostalism, there is a danger that this state of affairs might be perpetuated. It is possible rightly to stress the 'once-and-for-allness' of Pentecost, but at the same time to fail to grasp the divine programme for the Church in every age. We must not fail to emphasize that the power received by the Church at Pentecost may be received and known by the Church now, and that we cannot afford to be without it.

Without necessarily endorsing Pentecostalist theology, we must recognize that our Pentecostalist brethren frequently show a fervour and earnestness which are lacking in the older Protestant communions; and in prayerfulness, responsible giving and fellowship, some of them set an example to all. John Calvin is known as 'the theologian of the Holy Spirit', and as such he made a very considerable and positive contribution to the statement of the doctrine of the Holy Spirit. We, today, can do no less; and like Calvin we should be seeking to present a doctrine of the Spirit which is truly Biblical and which relates to the life and outreach of the Church. One thing is clear: the fulness of the Spirit is the Church's daily need. A powerless, languid Church is a sign of a fellowship unfilled by God's Spirit. But it is not the teaching of Scripture that the Church was meant to eke out a bare survival in a hostile world, holding a fort in conditions of siege. The enemy will not retreat before the preaching of a listless Church. The essential connection between the ministry of the Spirit and the preaching of the Church is all-important in the confrontation of evil powers. Paul asks, 'Received ye the Spirit by the works of the law, or by the hearing of faith?' (Gal 3:2). The connection between the preaching of the Gospel and the working of the Holy Spirit is unmistakable. The term 'the power of God' is applied both to Christ and to the preaching of the cross of Christ (Rom 1:16, 1 Cor 1:24). How vital, then, for the Church, in every age, to know the power and fulness of the Holy Spirit! The very power and defiance of the forces of darkness are a rebuke to the powerlessness and complacency of the Church, a complacency which regards revival as exceptional and lukewarmness as the to-be-expected! Until the Church begins to *think* differently, it is unlikely that her *experience* will be different.

Summary

Our practical conclusions may be briefly stated thus:

1. Deliverance from demon-possession must not be viewed out of the Gospel context in which, in the New Testament record, it is firmly set.

2. Mere exorcism, in whatever name, is condemned by our Lord. When there is *dispossession* of a demon, it can only be because there is *repossession* of the victim — i.e., by the Holy Spirit as Christ reigns in the heart.

3. The fact that some have exorcised demons in Christ's name, proves nothing in itself (Matt 7:22). Our standard for belief and practice is the Word of God alone. We cannot substitute any observed phenomena, and our interpretation of them, for this divinely given rule.

4. We are not asked to diagnose cases of supposed possession. It is much wiser and safer in such situations to rely prayerfully in faith upon the proclamation of the Word of God, witnessing to and praying for the sufferer.

5. Nothing less than the 'new birth' will meet the need of the demoniac or any other sinner. When this takes place the demon has been dispossessed. The only guarantee against possession is to be indwelt by the Holy Spirit, that is, to be 'born again'.

6. While a true believer, who is part of Christ's body and indwelt by the Spirit of God, cannot be the abode of a demon, our study has shown that he may be influenced by Satan and even become, for the time being, his unwitting tool.

7. When confronted by manifestations of demonic activity in a community, the Church should emphasize in her ministry the lordship of Christ, and especially His victory over Satan and his minions. If this goes out of focus in the mind and devotion of the Church, she will become enfeebled and afraid.

8. The whole Church is involved in the confrontation of satanic forces. If there is a crisis in missions today it is largely because there is a crisis of faith in the Church, and particularly in respect of the lordship of Christ. Yet where faithful witness and service are still found, even if fragmented, prayer and obedience will not be fruitless or in vain.

9. The worship of the Triune God through the risen Christ, and the proclamation of Christ's victory, are always infinitely stronger than all demonic forces in their strongest combinations.

10. Being 'filled with the Holy Spirit' is a prerequisite for service in an area where demonic presence is obvious, as indeed for all Christian service! It is unlikely that the forces of evil will retreat before carnal Christians.

The prayer of John Calvin well expresses the spirit in which we should daily seek to serve the Lord Jesus in this world:

'Grant, Almighty God, that as Thou art graciously pleased daily to set before us Thy sure and certain will, we may open our eyes and ears, and raise all our thoughts to that which not only reveals to us what is right, but also confirms us in a sound mind, so that we may go on in the course of true religion, and never turn aside, whatever Satan and his ministers may devise against us, but that we may stand firm and persevere, until having finished our warfare, we shall at length come unto that blessed rest which has been prepared for us in heaven by Jesus Christ our Lord. Amen.'[2]

2. *Commentary on Jeremiah*, Vol. 3, 197, 1950 edition, Grand Rapids.

EPILOGUE

While the Bible presents the Devil as a ruthless and cunning opponent, it abounds with words of comfort and reassurance for the Christian. Much of this comfort is found in the First Epistle of John. There we read, 'Greater is he that is in you that he that is in the world' (4:4). Yet while the apostle repeatedly assures believers of their safety in Christ, he warns against complacency. We must test the spirits and distinguish between the Spirit of truth and the spirit of error. This is the duty of each Christian as well as of the Church collectively. We must not be passive and idle when confronted by the instruments of the Devil, the false prophets and antichrists, but must counter their assaults with the proclamation of God's truth. We are to 'overcome' them (4:4). This can only be done in the strength and wisdom of our exalted Lord. Luther comments, 'It seems that those people (i.e., those who hold with antichrist) are the victors and that we are the vanquished. Therefore faith is needed. For we do not overcome with might and numbers; we overcome with faith and the Word.'[1]

While it is a mistake to become obsessed with thoughts about the Devil and his legions, it is equally foolish never to give him any thought at all. We must pray daily, 'Deliver us from the Evil One' (as Matthew 6:13 may be translated). Temptation is the work of the Devil, and it is against his arrows that we need divine protection. But the greatness of our adversary is seen particularly in his

1. *Lectures on The First Epistle of St. John*, Luther's *Works*, Vol. 30, Saint Louis, 1967.

'devices' or cunning designs (2 Cor 2:11), whereby he endeavours to 'get an advantage of us'. He does this when, for example, we harbour an unforgiving spirit, or when we would seek to obtain a worthy end by unworthy means.

The Christian is secure because he is indwelt by the victorious Saviour. He is free from the power and jurisdiction of Satan. 'The wicked one toucheth him not' (1 John 5:18). The word translated 'touch' means to grasp. Satan cannot recapture the man who is kept by Christ. In that sense the Christian is for ever beyond the reach of the Evil One. He is said to be 'of God' (1 John 4:4). The apostle writes, 'We know that we are of God' (1 John 5:19). And he places that statement in juxtaposition to the assertion, 'The whole world lieth in the wicked one.' The unbelieving world is in Satan's embrace, but the Christian is in the arms of the Saviour. Once he walked 'according to the course of this world, according to the prince of the power of the air, the spirit that now worketh in the children of disobedience'. Now he has been quickened by God's Spirit and walks in newness of life. No longer does he breathe the poisoned atmosphere of this world, an atmosphere impregnated with the serpent's venom. The Christian is begotten by God: the Evil One cannot lay hold of him.

In sharp contrast, the unbeliever is said to be 'of the devil' (1 John 3:8). He lives sinfully and in rebellion against God. This renders him a child of the devil (1 John 3:10).

The Apostle John, in his First Epistle, sees two families, 'the children of God' and 'the children of the Devil'. The one family is governed and moulded by the Devil whose evil character is stamped upon it. The other family is governed by God's Word and Spirit and it reflects the divine character. Those who are members of the family of God need not fear the Evil One. They are to be alert and watchful and clad in the armour which God supplies; but in Christ, their victorious Redeemer, they face the Devil and his dark angels fearlessly. As they abide in Christ and as Christ abides in them, and as in prayer they claim the promises of God, they stand invincible.

> *And Satan trembles, when he sees*
> *The weakest saint upon his knees.*

'For whatsoever is born of God overcometh the world: and this is the victory that overcometh the world, even our faith' (1 John 5:4). This faith, bestowed by a sovereign God, is not a brief candle that the wind blows out, but a fire that the storm only makes burn brighter.

APPENDICES

(A) *The Use of the word 'Satan' in Psalm 109*

The Apostle Peter, quoting from Psalm 109, says: 'Men and brethren, this Scripture must needs have been fulfilled, which the Holy Ghost by the mouth of David spake concerning Judas, which was guide to them that took Jesus' (Acts 1:16). It will not do to say, as some commentators have done, that Peter merely made a personal application of this psalm to Judas. Quite clearly he regarded it as a divine prophecy of his treachery and subsequent judgment.

In the sixth verse of this psalm we read: 'Set thou a wicked man over him: and let Satan (lit. an adversary; in the Septuagint it is *diabolos*) stand at his right hand.' The same expression, 'satan', is used in 1 Chronicles 21:1, in Job chapters 1 and 2, and in Zechariah 3:2. In these passages it is also translated 'Satan'. A number of commentators, including Calvin, Hengstenberg, Perowne, Delitzsch, Barnes, Leupold and Kirkpatrick, take the view that the expression 'satan' or 'adversary' in this psalm does not refer to the devil but to one of David's human adversaries like Doeg the Edomite or Cush the Benjamite. This interpretation they regard as better suited to the context. Thus this part of the psalm, with its scene of judgment, is regarded as a wish that retribution might overtake the chief offender (there is a transition in the psalm from many enemies to one enemy in particular) and that he might stand trial before a judge as heartless as himself and before a malicious and unscrupulous accuser. 'Appoint a wicked man over him and let an accuser stand at his right hand.' It is interesting to note the admission of Delitzsch that although, on his view, there is no direct reference to Satan here, there is a 'superhuman being' and he draws a parallel with the angel of Jehovah who 'stood in the way for an adversary (satan) against' Balaam (Num. 22:22).

Grammatically, and within the structure of the psalm in question, this understanding of the Hebrew word 'satan' is correct so far as it goes. There is no reason to reject the view that David had some human adversary in mind. David was profoundly conscious of the fact that he was anointed by Jehovah and he was jealous for God's glory. If his enemies were to pluck the crown from his head then God's name would be dishonoured and the faith of God's saints would be wounded. The motive of these imprecations is not to be found in any sense of private wrong or any desire for personal revenge, but in a real fear of seeing God's holy name blasphemed and His glory tarnished in the eyes of men.

But the view which limits Psalm 109 to David and one of his adversaries is altogether too short-sighted because it ignores the typical nature of David and his kingdom and overlooks the interpretation of the imprecatory psalms (all of which were written by David) in the New Testament, where their ultimate fulfilment is seen either in the judgment of Judas or in the apostasy of Israel (cf., Rom 11:9, 10). In the Christian Church Psalm 109 soon became known as the Psalmus Ischarioticus – the Iscariot Psalm. Whether, by rendering the verbs as futures, which may be done, the imprecatory psalms be interpreted as predictions rather than prayers, makes no moral difference. They remain psalms of Christ's holy judgment upon the impenitent in the manner defined in the New Testament. They belong to His passion and crucifixion.

We do not have to choose between an actual situation in David's life-time or a prophecy of a situation during Christ's earthly life; we may accept both. As William Binnie well says, 'Christ and Judas are present' in such psalms 'as truly as David and Ahithophel'. Once we place Psalm 109:6 against the background of the Christology and typology of the Psalter and within the framework of the infallible exposition of the 69th and 109th psalms which we have in Acts 1:16–20, we see that Luther is not so wrong as some expositors have suggested when he sees a clear reference to Judas in this text and to his captivation by the Devil. (*Works*, Vol. 14., p. 261. Concordia Publishing House, 1958.) Satan had become his counsellor and as such stood, so to speak, on his right hand. It was Satan who put it into the heart of Judas to betray the Master (Jn 13:2, 27).

The same view of Psalm 109:6 is taken by Matthew Henry (no mean expositor), George Horne and C. H. Spurgeon. The opinion of Hengstenberg that 'Satan is not elsewhere introduced in the psalms and a reference to him here could therefore be adopted only on forced grounds' really begs the question. Once we look at this statement of the psalm in the full light that Scripture throws upon it, there is no compelling reason for rejecting the conviction of Luther that ultimately the verse points us to Satan and Judas and is a prophecy of the doom of the latter.

(B) *Self-Induced Symptoms of Demon-possession*

It is worthy of note that the physical phenomena which appeared during the great spiritual awakenings of modern times, were sometimes self-induced by those who wished to be seen to be experiencing what was regarded as a divine blessing. Of the revival of 1739 Arnold Dallimore in his *Life of George Whitefield* writes: 'There can be little doubt that some of Wesley's people were influenced in these things by the French Prophets, for the self-induced paroxysm was a common practice among them.' Similarly in the Ulster Revival of 1859 there was often an expectation that conviction of sin would be accompanied by certain physical phenomena and thus there was aroused a desire to experience them. Consequently there were probably many instances of self-induced hypnotism ('sleeps'), and self-induced prostration. Some believers came to regard the prostrations as a mark of God's special favour, and, in spite of attempts to discourage them, wrought themselves into a state in which a sudden emotional collapse became almost inevitable. In great awakenings there have always been those who are genuinely overwhelmed in body and spirit by a sense of sin; but there are also those who themselves induce a pseudo-physical response, and others who, unsuspectingly, are used by the Devil to mimic the work of the Holy Spirit. In a culture which for generations has been steeped in the demonic, this is to be expected, and it would be perpetuated by the occurrence, from time to time, of actual demon-possession.

Similar distinctions between the real and the spurious have to be made in considering alleged demon-possession. Even in the evil physical phenomena witnessed in primitive societies, and associated by the people with Satan worship, the probability of occasional, or even frequent, cases of self-induced symptoms of possession has to be recognized.

The Christian worker who is faced with the physical phenomena associated with demonism, must bear in mind the possibility (a) of involuntary imitation, (b) of deliberate, self-induced imitation; both conditions being perpetuated by the occurrence, from time to time, of actual demon-possession. It may frequently be impossible to diagnose with any certainty in which of these conditions a person is to be classed, and this only serves to emphasize that the servant of Christ is not asked to diagnose alleged cases of possession, but to confront the demonic, whether it may express itself directly or indirectly, with the Word of the Risen Saviour and earnest prayer in His holy name.

It should also be remembered, in observing religious phenomena, that the possible operation of the power of mass hysteria, or, as it used to be called, the principle of sympathy, makes it exceedingly difficult *at the time*, to distinguish between the spiritual and purely psychological. The impulse of mass hysteria can be almost irresistible, as is witnessed by the behaviour of crowds in situations of riot and hysterical emotion. Archibald Alexander gives a striking example of this spirit influencing a congregation in his *Thoughts on Religious Experience*, 57f., Banner of Truth reprint, 1967.